PURE SOAPBOX

Merrell —

Carpé Diem!

PURE SOAPBOX

…a cleansing jolt of perspective, motivation, and humor

by

Kimberlie Dykeman

Wiggy Press

Wiggy Press an imprint of

Dalton Publishing

P.O. Box 242

Austin, Texas 78767

www.daltonpublishing.com

Printed in the United States of America

Interior design: Jason Hranicky

Cover Photography: Chad Duerksen, incidentimage.com

Cover design: Kenneth Ussenko, kuproductions.com

ISBN: 978-0-9740703-3-9

LCCN: 2008927480

ATTENTION ORGANIZATIONS AND SCHOOLS:

Quantity discounts are available on bulk purchases of this
book for educational purposes or fund raising.

For information, go to www.daltonpublishing.com

A portion of the proceeds from the sale of this book are
donated to the Lance Armstrong Foundation.

Thanks & Dedication

For those of you who have ever had to give an acceptance speech, let alone a little stand-up ditty at your own wedding, retirement, or Oscar party, you can certainly appreciate the challenge of remembering who to thank for helping you get there in one piece. God forbid, you forget your Uncle Joe or the third grade teacher you loved to hate! Well, multiply that anxiety by about 100 when it comes to acknowledging all the folks who have played some role in getting your book published! So, I shall cease with all the disclaimers and simply go for the obvious–and leave my number unlisted!

First off, God, you've laid out quite a journey for me. You bless me with the ability to bring great joy to others and ignite my pixie spirit to embrace each day with promise. This book is just another example of the power of belief.

In considering all that I have been blessed to accomplish, let alone all I intend to fulfill, I believe that the relationship with my family is the ultimate positive foundation for the go-getter I am today. They are the best cheering squad a gal could ever ask for –supporting and encouraging me to live my own life to its fullest! Not only do I give them praise and thanks, I dedicate this book to them as well.

Mom – No one understands me like you! You've given me the heart, spirit and breath to bring my dreams to life, and you inspire me more than you can ever imagine with your own life story. I love you and am forever jazzed to tell people that you're my very best friend!

Dad – Your strength and loving discipline have given me the wherewithal to do anything I put my mind to. Our bumpy past has taught us to cherish our future as truly great pals. I love you and I'll always be your "Scooter."

Natalie – We may still be polar opposites, but we've finally built a friendship I have prayed for my whole life. Your generosity is humbling and you have yet to realize just how special you are to the world. I love you! (Mom made me say it!)

Introduction

Welcome, to the little corner of my mind. A brilliant man named John Naisbitt once said, "The most exciting breakthrough of the 21st century will occur not because of technology, but because of an expanding concept of what it means to be human."

Folks, this concept has resonated in my noggin for years and eventually crescendoed into the driving force behind this book. To define this free-flowing discourse, I've coined the term "soapbox™" – an aerobic effort in and of itself – for it goes above and beyond the traditional connotation of an improvised platform from which folks eject opinions and prose.

Pure Soapbox…a cleansing jolt of perspective, motivation, and humor, an assemblage of virtual transmissions I have shared with clients, friends, and complete strangers across the country for years, serves as a forward-thinking showcase of candid wit and inspiration. Originally coined *The Monday Soapbox Edition*, each concoction has proven a readily devoured truffle of quotable common sense, oozing a Mary Poppins positive energy, yet delivered with a dash of New York, sarcastic flair, and a swift kick in the pants.

Serving as an ignition sequence to your back-burnered dynamic characteristics of human nature, *Pure Soapbox's* entertaining and stimulating observations will affect you with a rich under-conversation of life's profundity, irony, and sentiment.

Go ahead and dive in, folks, but prepare yourself for a good metaphorical cleansing. For I discreetly absolve myself of liability for the obscured truths you shall indeed face. Conversely, though, with acceptance speech in hand, I will shamelessly take credit for the glorious buried treasures you'll discover and confettied aha! moments you'll also joyfully experience. That said, I invite you to cleanse your palate, peer outside the proverbial box, and entertain the wondrous idea that *Pure Soapbox* will tattoo your memory and enhance your very state of being.

And, hey, worst case scenario, you've got one more for the magazine stack in the bathroom.

Yours in great spirit,

Kimberlie

PURE SOAPBOX

"ENTHUSIASM IS ONE OF THE MOST
POWERFUL ENGINES OF SUCCESS.
WHEN YOU DO A THING, DO IT WITH
YOUR MIGHT. PUT YOUR WHOLE SOUL
INTO IT. STAMP IT WITH YOUR OWN
PERSONALITY. BE ACTIVE, BE ENERGETIC,
BE ENTHUSIASTIC AND FAITHFUL, AND
YOU WILL ACCOMPLISH YOUR OBJECT.
NOTHING GREAT WAS EVER ACHIEVED
WITHOUT ENTHUSIASM."

~RALPH WALDO EMERSON

With a twinkle in your eye, no doubt you could regale your friends with a handful of fantastical life events that have unequivocally excited you; things that have forever captured your imagination and memory; things that you absolutely had to do or see or you would just die! (Honest!) You timed to iron out each particular detail, so, hopefully, everything would turn out just perfect, like your wedding, a long awaited vacation, a first date, an interview for your dream job, an Aerosmith concert. You know the feeling, the smile you wore from ear to ear, the memories you knew you'd have to share. Examine the painstaking preparation for each event, even if it only lasted two hours, and page through the spectacular stories that stemmed from it. Oh, the things we do for love…

Now, entertain applying that same enthusiasm toward an event called *your life*, purposefully and lovingly ironing out the critical details to ensure that you experience every

1

day to its fullest. Then strive diligently to create memories that transform this journey into the ultimate event. Just a matter of changing perspective, right? Well, hang on a sec, because simply sporting a smile ain't gonna make life one big carnival.

In truth, those critical details really comprise the collective health of your body, mind, family, relationships, and career. When they tilt out of balance, everything else is compromised, tarnishing your overall experience and quality of life. So, why wouldn't you be passionate about taking care of yourself, working on your relationships, driving towards your business goals, and ensuring a fantastic, long-lasting event?

Exude enthusiasm in creating your life. Don't just hang on for the ride. Be your own catalyst! Get fired up and make a difference in your own journey. Or, as my dear Dad so eloquently put it, "Don't drag your ass. The light ain't gonna get any greener."

"JUST DO IT!"

~NIKE

2

Here's one you can take to the proverbial bank. Sure, it's got a few cobwebs and reads quite trite, but that's par for the course. The best ones usually are. Just flip through the volumes of wisdom you've labeled "old fashioned" and tossed by the wayside. Now reflect on the times you found yourself muttering *hindsight is 20/20*, shaking your head and wishing you had listened. That said, read this one. Label it. Toss it. Lay it on someone else, and then forget it, at least for now. But mark my words, it will most certainly come back to either save you or haunt you like the rest.

Nike may have dibs on this phrase, and some of you may argue it lacks the luster it once had, but its inherent value remains intact when you distill its message. Make a choice to make a change. Stop thinking. Start doing. Stick to your guns. Follow your gut and…Go! Go! Go!

I'd wager you've logged quite a few conversations in which an authority figure or the guiding rules of the game kept you in line, pushed you to make decisions, or lit a fire under you for your own good. As adults, though, we find ourselves in equally countless situations where we unfortunately have no drill sergeant or good angel sitting on our shoulders telling us what we really should or shouldn't do. We find these defining moments in the making to be invariably saturated in irony and blind faith.

You'd probably have given your eyeteeth to have had someone behind you shouting, *"Just do it!"* as you hemmed and hawed over everything from what to have for breakfast to when to pop the big question. You find it even more frustrating when you humbly realize that the obstacle holding you back from success is none other than *you!* And isn't it funny that you're surprised, each time without fail, at the sense of relief and wondrous satisfaction that you enjoy *immediately* following the making of that dreaded decision?

Get it in gear, folks! Move forward to make things more black and white and steer clear of the quicksand of grey ambiguity and indecision. Plan your work, then work your plan. Listen to your heart. Fear less and risk more. *Just do it*, and watch how success makes a beeline right towards you.

"MAKE A CHOICE TO MAKE A CHANGE.
TODAY."

~KIMBERLIE DYKEMAN

Not just a catch phrase, gimmick, or ice-breaker, this commanding request clearly volleys the proverbial ball into your court. It proclaims that as you have the freedom to create the life you want to live, you're the only one who can ignite your intentions into action. Allow me to elaborate.

Picture a candle, a deceivingly simple package, filled with intoxicating fragrance, able to burn for umpteen hours, emit a stellar glow, change the atmosphere of a room or an entire evening, time after time, with but the strike of a match. Now, you can choose to let that candle sit and collect dust, never to release its wonderful aroma, light up a room, nor create ambiance for a night to remember. *Or,* you can choose to light that baby any chance you can and enjoy all it has to offer! Folks, that's a no-brainer, if I ever saw one.

You are that deceivingly simple package, filled to the brim with potential to be absolutely fabulous, unique, creative, enlightening, and successful. *You* have the potential to light up every room, every meeting, every workout, every weekend, every holiday, every goal, every client, every dinner party, every person you come across, every day. *You* have the opportunity and desire, the knowledge and resources, the abilities and God-given gifts to blossom into an amazing human *being*. You need only make one choice. Will you tap into and release your glorious potential, or will you keep it all bottled up, only to collect dust?

"Make a choice to make a change" simply reminds you that you are a born leader, decision maker, and winner. Not just today or tomorrow, but every day. I challenge you to ignite your spirited energy any chance you can. Change your bad habits or zip code, for that matter. Redecorate your office or wardrobe. Log five more minutes of cardio and one more hour of sleep. Renew your vows. Write your memoirs. Change your perspective. Hell, change your toothpaste! Embrace the endless possibilities and bask in the glow as you light up your own life.

4

"LIFE IS WHAT HAPPENS WHILE YOU'RE
MAKING OTHER PLANS.

~JOHN LENNON

...hang on, I'll be right back.

KD

"QUALITY IS NEVER AN ACCIDENT; IT IS ALWAYS THE RESULT OF HIGH INTENTION, SINCERE EFFORT, INTELLIGENT DIRECTION AND SKILLFUL EXECUTION; IT REPRESENTS THE WISE CHOICE OF MANY ALTERNATIVES."

~WILLIAM A. FOSTER

Question: When you put your name on something for the rest of the world to see, don't you usually make a concerted effort to make it sharp, memorable, beautiful, right-on, crisp, clean, and fabulous? You get the point. You try wholeheartedly to make it represent the quality of time and value you put into it, don't you?

Then it makes perfect sense to put your little heart into the one *thing* that carries the stamp of your name for an entire lifetime—*You!* Now, tell me why anyone would have a list of excuses, a mile long, for why they didn't try their best to make themselves sharp, memorable, beautiful, right-on, crisp, clean, fabulous, healthy, fit, and energetic for the rest of the world to see day after day after day?

If you've got one of those scrolls, here's the lesson of the day for you: People will remember the impact you have on them, the imprint you leave on their minds and hearts, because of the life you exude and lead. They'll soon forget the big deals you close, your fast car, expensive wardrobe, impressive career, and spotless house, but will long remember and appreciate your brilliant, healthy, lively and beautiful smile, attitude, body, point of view, personality, words of wisdom. Choose wisely, folks, by electing the alternative to wowing the masses with quality *stuff*; instead, wow them with a quality *you*, inside and out. Proudly post your name on the *you* that you've shaped, created, polished, and delivered to the world. And don't be shy to take all the credit!

"NEVER UNDERESTIMATE THE POWER WITHIN."

~ANONYMOUS

6

Some shmoe probably penned this random missive eons ago, without so much as a second thought. Nondescript in initial presence, it soon fills your belly with a growing warmth and hunger for more. The words command you to sit still and contemplate, even analyze the veritable mixed grill of experiences and escapades you've endured and enjoyed to attain the successes in your life. Moreover, it reminds you to forever dog-ear certain defining moments when you made a name for yourself, by leaving a lasting impact on those around you. Your personal humble history reveals an ever-powerful driving force that fuels your very essence and bears the name *inner strength*. Acknowledge it. Revel in it. Tap into it. And never underestimate it.

"THE BRAIN IS A WONDERFUL ORGAN; IT STARTS WORKING THE MOMENT YOU GET UP IN THE MORNING, AND DOES NOT STOP UNTIL YOU GET INTO THE OFFICE."

~ROBERT FROST

Now, now. I'm not targeting any one of you. That would be mean and way too easy! But, I just see some of you nodding in agreement. Not that you're a ding dong at work, but in the morning, it's all about you: getting *you* dressed, eating *your* breakfast perhaps with *your* loved ones, gathering *your* gear for the day. Then, once you step into *work mode* and high-tech, Corporate America autopilot takes over. For umpteen hours, it's all about work, getting the job done. Not until you return to Casa You do you switch gears back and remember yourself as a person with a name, a home, a family, an appetite, and a need for movement and rest.

Don't check your brain at the door, folks. Remember that your work is only as good as you are. So take care of yourself, acknowledge and honor your needs during the day. And when you get home at night, check your work and Big Brother at the door.

"THE DEFINITION OF UNHAPPINESS IS THE PERSON WHO DOESN'T KNOW WHERE HE'S GOING...AND IS WORKING HIMSELF TO DEATH TO GET THERE."

~ANONYMOUS

Know anyone who fits the bill here? Even one person is one victim too many. It's a darn shame what some people put themselves through, day in and day out, doing without true purpose or conviction. This gray area is just that, gray. Dull. Lifeless. Bogged down with a tremendous burden of uncertainty, emptiness, and lack of confidence. I suggest you steer clear of it.

Alas, not all circumstances lie within our collective control. So without judgment or agenda, I'll keep my insight simple: *Know why you do what you do*.

That's it, folks. That's my big tirade. My secret weapon for you. The hidden treasure. Have a *why* for your actions, from choosing what movie to rent, to what kind of business you intend to run, to which values you will uphold. Make a concerted effort to establish in your heart, mind, and spirit the unyielding reasons for the choices you make. Then witness the constructive clarity and relish the karmic relief that abounds from such a powerful action.

Find your *why*, my friends. Memorize it. Sleep on it.

Stick it on your fridge. Pour it in your coffee. Pump it into your car. Kvetch it on everyone around you. Tattoo it onto your forehead. Just find it. Oh, but take care. You might find yourself a bit happier. Then what'll you do?

"ALL OF US, IN THE GLOW OF FEELING
WE HAVE PLEASED, WANT TO DO MORE
TO PLEASE."

~WILLIAM JAMES

Compliments, positive feedback, thank yous, pats on the back are all such simple gifts. They cost nothing, are rarely overdone, never wasted, and can serve as dynamic forces in motivating those around us. A sincere acknowledgment and appreciation can penetrate even the thickest skins and noggins. And oftentimes, the transformation of your target—emotional outpouring, joyful expressions, or returned gratitude—will utterly amaze you. Those spontaneous reactions make you wonder why you ever hold back from sharing such electric thoughts.

Consider the countless friends, family members, co-workers, and near strangers alike who would benefit from your words of encouragement. Confetti them all generously and note how it comes back to you tenfold. We could all use a little more praise in our daily lives. And I'll bet the farm, folks, that if we sincerely lead by example, those around us will follow.

"ALL GROWTH IS A LEAP IN THE DARK,
A SPONTANEOUS UNPREMEDITATED ACT
WITHOUT THE BENEFIT OF EXPERIENCE."

~HENRY MILLER

Can I get an *Amen*?! Man, is that good! Amazing how such an uncomplicated, yet purposeful pairing of words can reignite the profound sensation of discovery, fear, and perpetual enlightenment we all experienced as little kids. I call this your *curiosity quotient*: That indescribable yearning for knowledge, newness, and surprise; that willingness to test drive without experience, to journey forward without direction, to jump into the proverbial spotlight without inhibitions.

As children we eat, sleep, and breathe it, then we *mutate* into adults! So many of us awaken to find ourselves in situations because of our personal, professional, or familial obligations, where we purposefully and painfully go out of our way to avoid rocking the boat. We work ourselves to death just to keep our sights narrowed on our own backyards, filled with that which we are familiar, can juggle, and, perhaps, can control. God forbid a curve ball gets thrown into the works, let alone, we allow our minds to wander and wonder "what if" or "why not."

Believe it or not, just peering over the barbed wire comfort zone of your current reality raises your curiosity quotient. In turn, you might then ponder the tethered state of affairs within the mossed-over walls. Do you dare stir up the daily minutia fogging the pillars of your temporal life? The 9-5 grind, beer and golf on Saturdays, scheduled fun with the kids on Sundays, the same treadmill routine, same breakfast, same date night, same family vacation, same circle of friends, same closet of clothes, same goals for the past 20 years. Are you asleep yet?

Maybe it's time you challenge yourself with all your senses to examine this recycled lifestyle with the same wonderment of what might need a little shaking up. Then take that next step and put thoughts into action. Become a kinetic *Being*. Turn your curiosity quotient up a notch. And *don't* stop to see if there's an owner's manual. *Don't* ask for directions. *Don't* worry about an audience. Savor the sizzle of spontaneity. Bask in the carefree sensation of renewed youth that ensues. And leap!

"THERE IS NO POINT AT WHICH YOU CAN
SAY, 'WELL, I'M SUCCESSFUL NOW. I
MIGHT AS WELL TAKE A NAP.'"

~CARRIE FISHER

Wouldn't that be fabulous? And wouldn't that have been a lovely standard if such a mentality had been applied to other benchmarks throughout our lives.

"I've graduated from high school. I might as well take a nap."

"I've hit my quota. I might as well take a nap."

"I've learned how to change the oil in my car..."

Yada, yada, yada.

Bottom line: It seems that every time we achieve a goal, pass a test, earn some merit, or simply figure something out, we find yet another challenge lurking behind Door #3. Maybe it comes out of left field and surprises the hell out of us. Maybe we assume that we've grown stronger and brighter, so we subconsciously search for successive tasks. Even still, perhaps, because we've titled ourselves the *King* or *Queen of Something Fabulous*, our audience now assumes we indeed *are* royalty and tosses us everything *and* the kitchen sink.

Herein lies your dilemma: Should you call it a day after you master the graceful art of flipping an omelet? Or, do you subscribe and surrender to the bigger-better-faster culture stacked with demands for over-achievement and delayed gratification?

Let me offer a paradigm shift: *Stop* thinking it has to be one or the other. *Stop* thinking there's only one right answer. *Start* thinking you can do both. Timing is everything and yet, day after day, week after week, year after year, you knock the bejeezus out of yourself to cram more into evenings out, business lunches, home projects, visits with your children; each time seemingly trying to outdo yourself because someone or something tells you that you have to.

Time out, folks! Take a baby step forward and try to pace yourself. Empower yourself by learning to say "when." In the end, this is not a race to the finish line. You don't have to set your pace of achieving, doing, winning, growing at full throttle. After all, he who finishes first is finished. (Maybe he should have taken a few more naps.)

"You are you, and you are unique. Anybody who gets to be with you, work with you or share your life with you is goddamn lucky."

~ Maria Shriver

12

Talk about a woman after my own heart! Pair this mantra with a power suit and a map of the world and there's nothing on that *List of Things to Conquer* that you can't bulldoze. Better yet, serve it up with your choice of whiskey or wheat grass, and you've got the perfect fix-a-flat for stress, cynicism, and self-pity.

I'll admit, perhaps this statement comes off a bit intense, some might even say a tad cocky. You certainly won't find it in a self-esteem starter kit. But whether you simply read it, mumble it with your morning java, or proclaim it daily with lungs filled and nostrils flaring en route to the office, you have the seed of its philosophy firmly planted in your psyche.

There is only one YOU. Period. End of sentence. You enter this world alone, must fend for yourself, and must make wise, calculative decisions to prove that Darwin was indeed right. And one element over which you possess inherent jurisdiction is who you permit into your personal society. Mind you, you may not gainfully orchestrate what role they'll play, but in the end, you are the omnipotent casting director.

Believe that *you* are unique, and the people surrounding you have a fabulous opportunity to observe, learn from, and experience you. In essence, you've invited them into the movie for free. When you set aside your second-guessing and allow this concept to fully permeate your humble heart and head, you'll see how truly powerful it is. *They* are the lucky ones, folks. *They* get to hang with the star!

I'll admit these rich truffles of idealism do indeed ooze a Mary Poppins kind of positive energy albeit delivered with a dash of New York attitude. So, I offer a bite-sized duo in which to indulge: Belief and Integrity. Give due diligence to these words and let their flavors consume your hungry palate. Put belief and integrity behind Maria's little mantra and allow the growth to begin organically. Soon you'll see yourself as the chanteuse, uniquely divine and wonderful, and center stage of your own little movie.

13

"ACT WITHOUT DOING; WORK WITHOUT EFFORT."

~TAO TE CHING

Did you ever push too hard only to have the metaphorical swing come back and hit you dead-on in the chin? Liken this to the self-inflicted searches for insight and inspiration from a bag of stale fortune cookies. Sometimes you've just got to let the meaning find you. Forcing profundity or comedy is like putting spoiled cream in your long awaited morning cup of coffee. It tastes like crap and wastes a perfectly good setup. Be you. Be open. And sip slowly.

14

"MOVEMENT IN A NEW DIRECTION HELPS
YOU FIND NEW CHEESE."

~HAW FROM *WHO MOVED MY CHEESE?*
BY DR. SPENCER JOHNSON

Make today the day that you plunge into uncharted territory. Purposefully cross paths with some of the sharpest strangers you will ever meet in your life. Throw a proverbial curve ball at your comfort zones and associate yourself with people from whom you can continuously learn about life on a daily basis. Scroll your picture show as ever changing and ever expanding.

No doubt, any and all of this sounds a little scary, like being strapped into a 24/7 roller coaster. But given a choice, I think you'd rather take that over *Groundhog Day* any day. The world offers so much out there for you to experience. You only need to open your minds. And, those of you who know of this quoted book are probably smiling right now, having another "a-ha!" or two. Just, think back to when peanut butter and jelly became old news. You have so very much to gain from even entertaining the idea of change, but trust me, it's even better when you let osmosis get the best of you. Choose to diligently and actively lay out a fabulous future. Choose to make each day's closing scroll of credits one that Spielberg would envy.

And understand that with change comes adventure and unpredictability with absolutely priceless rewards.

15

Embrace the indisputable fact that a plethora of super qualified people surrounds you. They're just itching to help someone, anyone, even YOU! This whole teamwork mentality is not just a lip service item served up by Mary Poppins, like HR Directors trying to win you over before you file a complaint. I know, I know, it is a very big deal, this "asking for help." For some of us, it isn't until everyone and their grandmother has their chance to smack us upside the head that we finally admit to abusing the *self-crowned* halo of Superwoman or Superman.

I'll bet quite a few of you are nodding and laughing as you see yourself in the same position. Labeling yourself the almighty Doler of Help, you seemingly take on the tasks of omniscience, omnipotence, and clairvoyance to boot. Well, I have news for you. Wayne Dyer says, "People treat us the way we teach them to treat us."

Have them think you're able to leap tall buildings in a single bound, and they'll ask you to perform such feats on a daily basis! Don't fear the reality that with only two hands, two legs, one brain, and a mere 24 hours a day, you simply do not have the ability to do it all. Furthermore, confess this simple fact and, believe it or not, people will not run in the opposite direction screaming!

Progress comes from the process, and we call this process reciprocity and outsourcing. Do what you can within your power, knowledge, time line, attention span, patience, and enjoyment, and engage others to help you. Yes, it takes time to drop off some of the weighty layers of responsibility. And, yes, you might think you're asking too much of others or freeing up too much time for yourself. But, trust me, your assigned helpers can handle it, and some day they, too, will go through the same process and call upon you for your big ol' brain work!

When you accept that there is no such thing as a truly self-made man or woman, the weight of the world seems a bit diminished. Remove the heavy "halo" of Wondergirl or guy, and your noggin will feel worlds lighter. Focus on what lies within your scope of sanity and strength. While you're at it, try sitting on the sidelines. Toss out thoughts, questions, and ideas for someone else to transform into the fruition of a project for which you'd still be reading the cake box directions. Gather 'em up and farm it out! Purposefully creating synergy with significant pivotal people will catalyze, unify, and unleash the greatest potential within and between you and them. Invariably these relationships benefit everyone on board, and success becomes a daily dessert.

"IF YOU CAN DREAM IT, YOU CAN
DO IT."

~WALT DISNEY

16

Think of the many encounters you've had with society's special individuals, colloquially labeled *the dreamers*, the supposed starving artists, wannabe actors, natural born tinkerers and concoctors of useless gadgets. In short, we say they are the eccentrics, with their heads in the clouds, floating along in their protective bubbles, doing work most of us call play, surrounded by things only a child could appreciate. I find it amusing how quickly we judge these people, assuming they possess no true sense of responsibility beyond themselves, have no clue how to use a laptop, and certainly have no sense of time or urgency.

Oh, but give these so-called silly fools a second glance and you might notice some of their other standout qualities that you find yourself lacking. You may wonder, "Where do they get all that energy? What's the secret to their success? Why are they so laid-back? What do *they* know that I don't?"

Let me propose an answer. Ironically, without their knowing it, these geniuses have tapped into the intriguing field of study called psycho-neuro-immunology. (Stay with me.) Their vivid imaginings and incessant pursuit of wonderful, impossible dreams yield the fabulous physiological side effects of reduced stress, tip-top immune systems, and enough positive energy for a small Italian village! Garnish that with an unyielding excitement for chaos and an ethereal stroke of flair and you've got another Edison, Klimt, or Churchill on your hands.

Simply put, dreams hold the key. They open the secret conduit to transport us back to our childhoods. They lead us right back to the highs of thinking outside the box, where we find laughter, peace, passion, resiliency, and absolute dynamic energy. Dreaming provides the safe way to test-drive the possibilities for the future, for we cannot fail in the abyss of imagination. There is no right or wrong there. No one lecturing, "It can't be done." No such thing as a timeline, deadline, or glass ceiling.

Sounds like a no-brainer to me. *Now* who looks a little foolish? Lucky for you, though, buried beneath the diurnal details of your j-o-b, family responsibilities, and moral obligations awaits a rickety, disheveled sense of purpose just jonesing for the oil can. I'm also willing to bet that you'll relocate a rich sense of humor, a few untapped talents, a thirst for discovery and challenge, and a list of outrageous daydreams socked away since you became an adult. And you wonder why you've felt a little bogged down! All that organic, good-stuff tends to grow into a burdensome bag-o-composted-guilt if you never let it out to bloom.

Perhaps it's time to aerate your noggin. Give yourself permission to invest in your passions, drives, and dreams, and watch your *self* change from the inside-out. *This* is the secret to high-energy living. Even if not-a-one of your wish list items ever comes to fruition, in the end, my friends, it's the journey, not the destination, that mattered all along. And you can always dream *another* little dream. Remember there are no rules. No one is keeping score. And the audience of one will never walk out on you.

17

"ALL THE ANIMALS EXCEPTING MAN
KNOW THAT THE PRINCIPAL BUSINESS
OF LIFE IS TO ENJOY IT."

~Samuel Butler

Ain't that the truth! I'll wager that you scarcely remember the last time you cashed in a handful of your jillion backlogged sick days for some blissful R&R. And invariably, when you harken back to those retreats that were filled with unadulterated fun, you wonder, under furrowed brow, why you needed to convince yourself that you had to "earn" this time of rest. What are you saving up for anyway? Need I remind you that you can't take it with you when you go?

That said, perhaps it's time for a fresh look at an old, and often overlooked vocabulary word. Say it with me, now:

va•ca•tion *(Va*ca'tion) n.* A period of time devoted to pleasure, rest, or relaxation.

Unfortunately, some of you have forgotten the definition of this pleasurably promising word, let alone how to use it in a sentence. If you find you qualify as one these vocab-deficient, self-neglecting workaholics, there's no need to identify yourself or say five "Hail Kimberlies."

Just get off your can and vacate the premises, folks! Be it for a week or a wink, allow yourself the time off and time out. You are fabulous just as you are, and therefore you have earned it. Don't merely survive. Thrive! We are all in the business of living first. And business is *goood*!

"The whole life lies in the verb seeing."

~Teilhard de Chardin

It all comes down to one fabulously, all-encompassing word: *Perspective*. A tunnel view of life can prove overwhelming, and yet dangerously boring. The old adage of not seeing the forest for the trees comes to mind. And, at times, the projection may appear scattered, fuzzy, or closed-off and oscillating with a drowning drone. Staring into the abyss of banality, we often overlook our basic need to retreat in order to re-acknowledge the world's powerful productions of innate order, natural beauty, and diversity within reason.

Trust that this is all part of the game of life: We start off safe by learning the rules of Black-and-White, and then a flickering of circumstances teaches us to colorfully bend them. And, Voila! We see the revelation of a whole new network and stand amazed at what the right sides of our bitty brains have withheld from the big screen! Seizing the plentiful opportunities to see the other side or view a fresh angle makes the experience of life so un boring, un-static, and un-complicated, we kick ourselves for forgetting how spectacular it really is. An ironic sense of peace comes from the excitement of seeing something for the first time... again. People, places, things, events, memories, dreams—they all take on a new hue, a new hum, a new fragrance, a new meaning.

Perhaps this is the prescription we need lying right at our fingertips, which no pair of specs can emulate: A remedial looking glass that brightens these sights with High-Def color and showcases their ultimate value and vitality. So stand up, sit down, lean, squint—geez—poke and prod for all I care! But make a choice to adjust the volume, the brightness, the contrast, or the whole darn channel. You've been given the best subscription in town, folks. Don't just stick to the reruns.

"LIFE'S A JOURNEY, NOT A DESTINATION."

~STEVEN TYLER, *AEROSMITH*

Hey there, rock and rollers! Here's a simple yet profound riff from the Canon of the music underworld. A hidden treasure from one of the disciples of lyric and noise that needs no explanation, no elaboration, and no drum roll.

Indeed, one of the great poets of our time enlightens us with a flick of his mic and a howl from his chops. Not bad for a stoner of the seventies, huh? Deceivingly basic at first glance, you must step back to appreciate its expanding profundity and note how it levels the playing field in one fell swoop. With commonsensical clarity it serves to remind us that we are all on the same map, folks. So, enjoy the route, the scenery, the pit stops, the landmarks, heck, even the 7-11s along the way. Take it all in before someone folds it all up.

"NECESSITY IS THE MOTHER OF INVENTION."

~ANONYMOUS

20

Ain't it the truth? Still, I'll withhold from blowing sunshine with the making lemonade aphorism. Instead, let's stretch this a bit and wrap it in a more user-friendly package. How about...*People will make changes when sufficiently disturbed*. Here's where I'm going with this.

I find it absolutely amusing how, as creatures of habit, we spin intricately protective webs around our worlds. We find sanctuary within our little palaces, purposefully avoiding upset within our shielded strategy of who we know, where we go, what we have and give, and what we believe to be the truth. What's fabulously intriguing about this setup is that we figure out what works for us, then toil our butts off to keep everything on an even keel. The old adage, *if it ain't broke, don't fix it*, surely comes to mind, and I applaud folks who achieve such a coveted state of homeostasis. Truly, I do.

But, it's also tremendously frustrating to observe those who blindly believe their ample supplies of everything-I-need-to-survive snack packs will last forever, undisturbed and perfect in their own right. Truth be told, their masterminded systems of safety will get shaken up, drop-kicked, even blown to bits at some point when life pitches a curve ball or two. An unexpected person, place, thing, or event crosses home plate and all of a sudden the rules change, and the game gets exciting!

When it does, the ill-prepared struggle to get by, for they naively tag change as something that's "not for me." The hiccup now morphs into a mountain of profanity, indecisiveness, and fear.

On the other hand, those players prepared to tread these unruly waters, tap their brains, ask for help, and attain resolution through assimilation and enlightenment.

So I ask you: How tightly have you weaved your web? How far into the box have you cornered yourself? If all hell broke loose tomorrow, could you do the math or would you freeze up?

A bit much? Well, tough. The opening quote may have only been five words long to start with, but it needed expansion. Still, if you insist on a summary, here's the slow pitch.

It's *okay* to create, download, upgrade, and re-create your Program of *Me*. But prepare for the inevitable virus or two, or 5,000, which can and will find their way into your mainframe. Believe in yourself and build trust in the umpteen brilliant resources readily available to you, some of which just might be the perfect puzzle-fit to the new version of you.

"DON'T COMPROMISE YOURSELF. YOU
ARE ALL YOU'VE GOT."

~JANIS JOPLIN

Here's a tasty one-liner for you to gnash on. Take your time with it and be sure to wash it down with a smooth chaser. It emerges from the kitchen of another extraordinary creator, whose chops could shake-n-bake music with unique flavor and flair of the times. Given the chance, the resounding simplicity of this thought will pepper your tongue as you fight the urge for seconds. I only hope it leaves an uncomfortable burning in your belly that will continually remind you of the gravity of the message transpiring here.

"ALL THE SAME, WE TAKE OUR CHANCES, LAUGHED AT BY TIME, TRICKED BY CIRCUMSTANCES. PLUS CA CHANGE, PLUS C'EST LA MEME CHOSE. THE MORE THAT THINGS CHANGE, THE MORE THEY STAY THE SAME."

~GEDDY LEE & JEAN-BAPTISTE ALPHONSE KARR

Stumble through this quote, and you'll swear Yogi Berra concocted yet another puzzler. But, for the record, the real penning poet fronts the Canadian band Rush, whose creations still complex the airwaves. And though the labyrinth of lyrics wax ironic, this guy nailed the undercurrent of life in one fell swoop. Change and her relentless rhythm unashamedly convicts and collectively connects us as we stand in awe of the seeming bombardment of negative events that the past decade has delivered: The tragedy of 9-11, the failing markets, the additional violence throughout America, the war in Iraq. You name it and it's more than just front page worthy. And as the media cumulatively frightens the bejeezus out of us, many of us find ourselves *re*-evaluating, *re*-booting, and *re*-promising to *re*-unite and make this world a better place. Geez, what's the scurry all about, now? Why are we feverishly trying to concoct our own band-aid therapy, while still fearing that the worst has yet to come down on us?

Whether it's 2001 or the 1930s, the barefaced backdrop may have changed, as have the countless events of devastation, but we as a nation remain the same. We're all still just a bunch of folks living on a big plot of land called America. That said, there has never been a *right time* to share fellowship, take care of each other, go to church, invest in ourselves, our families, and our businesses; respect our elders, donate to charities, take time off, question our value system, show our emotions, pray for one another, or stand together. *Every day* is the *right time.* So, fling open the doors, settle down and keep the home fires burning. Change your perspective and, believe me, you'll see how it doesn't really matter where your assigned seat is.

23

Oy vey! Ever had one of those days, weeks, months, or dare I say, years when you'd like to throw in the towel, slap the Murphy's Law label across your forehead, and wash it all down with a cold beer and a box of Hot Tamales? You know what I'm talking about. When your gloomy *Groundhog Day* world lines your days with an incessant stream of obstacles, seemingly presenting themselves in a choreographed, *Catch-22* pattern.

You humbly take up arms and fight for your cause, yet you barely catch a break to relish the joy in overcoming one challenge when another slips right in to assume its position and throw you for another loop. Person, place, thing, you name it, it fronts a mile-long deli line of things you must initiate and duplicate; battle and coddle; learn, teach, fix, change, add and delete—just to get you one measly inch closer to your goal. Alas, the "poor me" cloak weighs you down to a crawl, right? Well, try this one on for size:

"THE RUNG OF A LADDER WAS NEVER MEANT TO REST

UPON, BUT ONLY TO SUPPORT YOU LONG ENOUGH TO ENABLE YOU TO REACH FOR SOMETHING HIGHER."

~Thomas Henry Huxley

Try tilting your game board about 90 degrees. Now instead of seeing such challenges on a linear plane, one following in line after the other, you create a clear view of these curve balls and lessons learned for their true fundamental, albeit unforgiving, purpose: Cumulative steps leading to a lifesaving summit. None are ever the same, nor do they carry the same weight, affect the same response, or bring about the same resolution or growth. That said, the recovery time following each may then be as short as a flip commercial or as long as a politician's term. Either way, you must giddy-up, shake it off, psyche yourself up for the next wave, and move on and up. That's right...on and up. To the next rung. You are all brilliant contenders in your own right, gaining power and strength at each new level. Commit yourself to the climb and you'll never be overcome.

24

"IN A RELATIONSHIP, TWO HALVES
DON'T MAKE A WHOLE. TWO WHOLES
MAKE A WHOLE."

~JO COUDERT

Attached at the hip. Funny little phrase, isn't it? Perhaps you reading this book creates a linking of sorts, an attachment or connection that makes us need the other to infuse and illuminate our own Big Picture, whether of the day, an idea, a dream, a lifestyle, or a lifetime.

Moreover, I metaphorically propose that each of us embodies a full 24-pack of Crayola crayons. Plenty of variety there to play with, right? Boasting all the colors of the rainbow, and then some, and uniformly brimming with gorgeous pigment that defines our every thread and thought. *Oooooh*, but remember what the full set of 48 looks like? Not to mention 64 or 128! Fluorescents, metallics, unpronounceable shades of blue, green, and brown, and every color word combo imaginable. Not that more is better, nor is the littlest pack incomplete, less than half, or even limited. But the end result, the picture creatively born from the bigger, more varied palette, climbs to a colorfully dramatic new dimension: A Crayola masterpiece of Manet or Klimt proportion.

Truth be told, folks, even if your collection is peeled down to the labels and worn down to nubs, 24 is, was, and always will be complete and unlimited by design and definition. Make this simple yet crucial connection and you just might begin to see both yourself and those in and around your life as complete creations, absolute sets. Playfully and boldly blend with family and friends, sweethearts, co-workers and strangers, and discover the magical cornucopia of shades you can add to this work of art called life.

"I DON'T BELIEVE IN BEATLES. I JUST
BELIEVE IN ME."

~JOHN LENNON

Aaaahhh, yes, here we have another anecdote from yet another pioneer of timeless society who embodied greatness both with and without his band of brothers.

Indeed we are all part of some larger entity— friendship, family, a team, organization, corporation, or perhaps even book-of-the-month club or rock-n-roll band. The list scrolls endlessly. You could plug yourself into a jillion partnerships for reasons of acceptance, recognition, money, accountability factors, social aspects, personal rewards, hell, even just to say you are a member of something!

So, take a moment and think about why you still proudly carry the virtual membership card for each. I hope that when all is said and done, regardless of whatever bonuses you reap from such fellowships, you realize that *you* are the magical ingredient in each entity.

The fact is you get what you give once you acknowledge the absolute greatness that you embody simply as a solo artist. Trust in your uniqueness, that these outside affiliations stand secondary to the ultimate union between you and your true heart. Give yourself "buy-in" first, then decide where your music might turn symphony— and plug in! Belief is an extremely powerful instrument, provided you learn how to play it.

26

Hello and welcome to the flashback hour.

I find it funny how obscure parts of conversations sneak up on you days or weeks later, never really following a pattern of topic or timing. Perhaps something in your noggin elected to dog-ear a convolution for future reference. Perhaps the moment you heard the words, something inside you acknowledged the gravity of the text and knew its worth would grow exponentially if socked away to fully ripen.

Point being, I had an "a-ha" today when a bookmarked selection was imported to the front page, so-to-speak, and it made me feel fabulous. A few weeks ago someone told me that I was brave and had great courage. I know it sounds so very simple, but I can't remember anyone ever saying such a thing to me. And, regardless of the expanse of the conversation, that compliment has stayed afloat in my mind, yet back-burnered until just yesterday. And today I thought of the concept of bravery and courage and how it is rarely shared, discussed, or given limelight, probably because we need to personify it to make it a true

47

member of our treasure chest of choice vocab. Perhaps an introduction will affect a rediscovery of her value and promise.

> "Courage looks you straight in the eye. She is not impressed with power trippers, and she knows first aid. Courage is not afraid to weep, and she is not afraid to pray, even when she is not sure whom she is praying to. When she walks it is clear she has made the journey from loneliness to solitude. The people who told me she was stern were not lying; they just forgot to mention that she was kind."
>
> ~J. Ruth Gendler

Regardless of the word, or thought or question, when you allow the flashback to step into your scope again and bloom, you'd be amazed at the insight you can gain. The *why* behind this is an ever-changing current reality and a powerful mind-link to the past that serves as a lesson plan.

"HAVING A DREAM THAT YOU DON'T PURSUE IS LIKE BUYING AN ICE CREAM CONE AND WATCHING IT MELT ALL OVER YOUR HAND!"

~ANONYMOUS

So, what'll it be, folks? Chocolate or vanilla? Or a stack of napkins?

KD

28

There's nothing quite like stepping out of your familiar toiling environment, away from no-brainer, diurnal activities, and into a different space in time. Upon returning to your "two eggs over easy, side of bacon, and burn the toast" home base, your perspective is undoubtedly refreshed, perhaps more colorful, perhaps more dynamic.

Those random junkets serve to simply affirm a heart-warming thought that you certainly live a blessed life and are in the right place, at the right time, with the right people surrounding you, right now. On the other hand, though, the change of scenery may tell you just the opposite and prompt you to hit the eject button from a time, place, and people that limit your coveted peace of mind.

Regardless of the story's ending, the trip didn't make your 9-to-5 life any more fabulous or horrendous. You changed your perspective to have it mean more in relation to your little bubble of life. And who's to say your vacation was only in your mind?

RECIPE: "GIVERS GAIN."

~FROM THE KITCHEN OF: *ANONYMOUS*

Gather 'round. Today I come to you with a simple thought, so un-stuffed and un-fried and pleasantly filling, that none of you can plead heartburn after its consumption. Alas, my hungry dinner guests, we're going right for the main course!

Perhaps you've heard of this recipe from your dear Mom's teachings, the Bible, an organization's mission statement, or an old crooner's tale. But regardless of the source, the cooking directions remain unvaried across the board and oh-so-user-friendly:

1. Give unto others

2. Receive and be thankful

Prep time: None

Serving size: Immeasurable

Yields: Countless

As for the RDA of servings, I don't think a big enough pyramid exists. And honestly, who really needs one?

We interrupt your life to bring you the following:

"Significant conversations build relationships."

~Anonymous

30

We are having a conversation right now. Each email you have received from your co-workers, your friends, that pain-in-the-ass Real Estate guy who keeps spamming you has been a conversation. Each seminar, piece of mail, memo, gossip session, dinner-date, meeting, and "Hi, honey, I'm home," equals a conversation. And in each case, the messages delivered, inferred, interpreted, or perhaps, lost, held some degree of importance, for they hit their target—*you*.

That said, I have a simple message: Pay attention. Pay attention to the impact of the barrage of messages that flurry around you day-in and day-out. The ones you choose to toss literally or figuratively out the window were probably either low-price items in the first place or shamefully under-delivered. Bottom line: No further thought elicited, let alone follow-up or parting gift for the bearer.

Aaahhh, but then you may savor the celebrated golden nuggets of conversations that present themselves in fabulous packaging. They shine on your current reality, perhaps leave residual warmth, and spark your curiosity with an intangible under-conversation. These exchanges leave you wanting more and change your very being. Again, pay attention to these conversations because they build and sustain the relationships that keep you alive. Follow the ornate trail leading to the person or people responsible, and you'll learn that they invariably feel and think the very same way. Nurture and grow these relationships with appreciation, respect, and love. They are significant and deserve nothing less, and neither do you.

"HAPPINESS IS NOT A GOAL,
IT IS A BY-PRODUCT."

~ELEANOR ROOSEVELT

3 1

Pull up an eggnog and hear me out.

And so begins the once-a-year mad rush. The hunt for the perfect gift. Fighting crowds for last minute preparations. Those of us not hurrying home for Christmas are cramming in last minute get-aways. 'Tis the season of joy and merriment, now on sale for $69.99, aisle 5. Alas, the holiday spell rears its alter-ego, Hallmark-ed ugly head. From the sounds of it, you'd think we were readying ourselves for the fight of a lifetime, damned and determined to make this celebration more memorable and more star-studded than the last. But this year's traditionally frantic, albeit festive holiday season is decorated in a different set of lights.

Unfortunately, some of us find ourselves, yet again, up against bosses and bills, deadlines and waiting lines. Ironically, this time of supposed glee surfaces another year's memories, sweet and bitter alike. Earning its own chapter in our collective personal history books, sometimes we stand in awe of the tough times and negative events that altered the very backdrop of The Big Picture. Many of us even take to re-evaluating, re-booting, and re-uniting in hopes of making the neighborhood, let alone this world, a better place.

But to our dismay, the pressures of our bigger-better-faster high-tech society yank our global gaze back to an unyielding state of chronic stress. Weighed down, perhaps, by the loss of family, friends, jobs, and financial security, our ability to regain a natural balance stands compromised, and we wonder what can transform this into a happy holiday again.

Well, if the glass appears half-empty, I can tell you right now, if you pray each year that good ol' St. Nick will overstuff your stocking with happiness, you might as well ask for a Lego erector set to go along with it. For, I have a hunch that you'll need a few colorful tools, and perhaps the magic of Rudolph's shiner, to bring this intangible notion into sight as a sparkly new toy under the tree.

With little reservation, I propose that a wish for a state of equilibrium tops our common holiday lists. So perhaps this is opportunity knocking, egging you to take the reins and pursue your own path toward surviving and thriving. Admittedly, giving to others is paramount on your mind, but if you're yearning for a healthier state of mind and for the clouds to clear, you've got to give to yourself. And time is of the essence. When you re-learn how to take care of and reward yourself, your valuation of self in relationship with everything and everyone around you will profoundly change, and you'll find your needy glass filled with the spirits of true joy.

You have the power to dictate your experience during the holidays. You must make it a time of relaxing, reflecting, and rejoicing in how far you've come each year in all aspects of your life. If you fail to give to yourself, you'll rob yourself of the opportunity to attain balance and genuine happiness and embrace the coming of a healthy new year.

32

Beware! This one might sting a bit...but I do it out of *looooove*.

Truth be told, somebody out there, whether in the office next to you, or on the other side of the globe, has you beat. Whether in the area of health, wealth, wisdom, skills, or achievements, I'm willing to bet you can find thousands who stack up measurably head and shoulders above your Guinness-Book personal best. You say you've won the Nobel Peace Prize or an Olympic gold? Think you're all-that-and-a-bag-of-chips at parallel parking, omelet flipping, or joke telling? Sorry, folks, but someone has probably mastered it better than you.

Now, before you get bent out of shape thinking that I have pawned my evil alter ego on you, I'm also willing to dig into my Louis Vuitton bag of articulation and deliver two words in self-fulfilling rebuttal: BIG DEAL! Or perhaps you prefer the soft-serve version to a one-two-punch:

"WE CAN DO NO GREAT THINGS; ONLY SMALL THINGS WITH GREAT LOVE."

~SAINT MOTHER TERESA

59

Closing the deal-of-the-century because your fragile corporate behind was on the line isn't all it's cracked up to be, n'est-ce pas? Especially when you would have traded it in a heartbeat to spend those lost weekends with your family, helping out your friends, or taking up golf—for the third time. The level of greatness we tattoo on the things we acquire, the ranks we climb, prizes we win, skills we perfect, people we affect, or movements we inspire exist relative to the next guy's book of lists. And worst of all, we always find the bar a bit higher the next time out. The real problem here, though, rests in our allowance of society to price tag our lives.

But, hang on; hang on. There spins a loophole, my friends. Rub your eyes and take a peek through a different colored lens and pluck out the real shining gems that reflect the great love you put into each. I'll wager that these golden nuggets take on the nondescript shape of a quirky acquired ability, a commonplace idea, a not-so-glamorous job, and perhaps an overlooked gift or outdated flair for the eccentric. All of which deflect any label, for their true value is priceless, intangible, and seemingly limitless in their ability to elicit yet another smile, a-ha, or thank you.

Needless to say, this concept has been baked, frosted, and served up in a myriad of flavors, but the under-conversation flows from the same ingredient: Greatness in your life will flow from whatever warms your heart. See if you can get your arms around that one!

"THE MOST EXCITING BREAKTHROUGH
OF THE 21ST CENTURY WILL OCCUR
NOT BECAUSE OF TECHNOLOGY, BUT
BECAUSE OF AN EXPANDING CONCEPT
OF WHAT IT MEANS TO BE HUMAN."

~ JOHN NAISBITT

Question: When's the last time you elected to take time off from the chaotic, daily drudgery of *The Box*, arguably labeled the Infinite Advancement for the Good of Mankind? Does your computer-parked keister need a time-out from this aggravating, yet invaluable conduit to the masses?

Hopefully, every once in a while, you experience an "a-ha" that prompts some kind of ritual unplugging from your technologically intoxicated zone. And, hopefully it's by choice, not coyly calendared in, or the side effect of a blasted blackout. In timing-out from inanimate gear and tuning-in to a live, responsive audience, you acquiesce to the back-burnered spiritual demands of human nature. Hope and fear, connection and longing, love and forgiveness, nature and spirituality are all revived. So how do you integrate this high-touch lifeline with a high-tech lifestyle?

As simple living beings, we need to honor the irrefutable fact that just as we stand subject to weaknesses, imperfections, and fragility, we brim with gifts, emotions, thoughts, and aspirations that just can't be appreciated by an inert object, over a 30-second phone call, or via email. Go ahead and enjoy the fruits of cutting-edge advancements, my wired Websters, but pair them with the relationships that ground you as walking, talking, playing, laughing, feeling, questioning human beings.

Embrace the dynamic opportunity to evolve your self-culture by balancing the immeasurable power of technology with the inherent needs of people as people. You are equally worthy, needed, and loved, but will regrettably never realize your true potential if computerized culture gets the best of you, and your family and friends only get the rest.

"TWENTY YEARS FROM NOW YOU WILL BE MORE DISAPPOINTED BY THE THINGS THAT YOU DIDN'T DO THAN BY THE ONES YOU DID DO. SO THROW OFF THE BOWLINES. SAIL AWAY FROM THE SAFE HARBOR. CATCH THE TRADE WINDS IN YOUR SAILS. EXPLORE. DREAM. DISCOVER."

~MARK TWAIN

34

May I be the millionth fool to suggest you only live once; hindsight is 20/20; carpe diem; live and learn; better to have loved and lost. Feel free to babble on with your own.

My, my, how frustratingly uncanny 'tis the myriad aphorisms advertising insight and advice. Their collective foreshadowing has been laid earnestly before our scurrying feet, only to be embraced a moment too late or a lifetime long gone. May I suggest then, that you review the memoirs of the past few months, if not the past few years of your life under the analytical scope of the Ghost of Christmas Past. Yank out the lost opportunities, the woulda-shoulda-coulda's, and the wishes of what might have been, and ask yourself *why*?

Challenge yourself with the unambiguous notion that you are blessed with a resounding, intrinsic ability to alter the course of your life. Then take the reins and giddy-up, for cobwebs and moss have never been in style, and people will offer you just so much cheese to go with your *whine*. Choose a path of least resistance, albeit with galumphing and guesswork, but trust that the adventures you'll find diving into the abyss of discovery are well worth the nails you'll bite and the *Tums* you'll devour.

"To have the sense of creative activity is the great happiness and the great proof of being alive."

~Matthew Arnold

The time has come to resuscitate the rare moments when you seemingly stepped out of your judgmental self, away from your ego, and allowed the kid in you to take over. Perhaps you loudly gesticulated, cracked a few jokes, or played hooky. In open confession, I'll bet you caused a little ruckus, some blushing embarrassment, and even made a mess. Each seamless integration into the environs, movement, and possibilities shunted your essence with breath, pulse, and effervescent giddiness.

Tossing care to the wind never felt so *gooood*, right? Well then, simmer with these fleeting yet fabulously freeing experiences a bit longer and let the colorful juices of your right brain stew in even more spice.

Kick off the heels, Lola! Loosen your tie, Mr. Smith! Yank your glazed gaze from the electro-magnetic enigma and allow the nervous energy, warm fuzzies, and goose bumps of those lapses to envelope your very being. Fifty bucks says you're intoxicated by the shades, the textures, the aromas, the flavors, and even the emotions as if you were still there in those priceless, captivating moments.

Ahhhhhhh.

Well, here's a news flash: You can experience this sensational joyride each and every day. No vending machine or delivery guy required—this stuff is never out of stock!

Jump in this very minute and confetti your daily life with the energy of this childlike exhilaration. Choose creation over manipulation, change over fear, flair over familiarity, and animation over head trip. Drop the act of dissecting the butterfly on the wheel, pay attention to the eminent ball in your court, and take a stab at the three-point shot to win the game.

"A BIRD DOESN'T SING BECAUSE IT HAS
AN ANSWER, IT SINGS BECAUSE IT HAS
A SONG."

~MAYA ANGELOU

36

And so it begins with beauty of submission. It is with refreshed energy and emancipation that I deliver this compilation, praying it prevails over the litany of taxing and trite amalgamations that litter your desktop. With great anticipation, yet transient restraint, I have listened and honored the lingering under-conversation in my pea-pod brain. And the results rouse a recurring mission to depict and entertain with humor, to prompt and effect with profundity and sentiment. Yet, the deliberate transmission of text is not the music, my friends. Instead, the jazz and groove eclipse the rind and resonate an essence that invigorates me. Effectively, the words write me.

And so I must ask, where lies equal enjoyment in your existence? What fills your belly with glee and moves your lips to hummmm your very own anthem? Does your spirit-soaked, sense of purpose take shape in the flesh? Have you clipped it to your lapel, a beaming brass broach for the curious world to see and admire? If so, then keep that baby shining! However, if your jewel be hidden, perhaps you'll reconsider the consequences of hindsight.

I say, become an ambassador to your song, folks. Dispense of the knee-jerk deflection of feelings and release your music. Course osmotically through the labyrinth of the tangible and take to galumphing outside the proverbial box of society's expectations. Dig up a sidelined story, tap your historical humble beginnings, or soapbox your own fellowship of family, friends, and colleagues. Move to be moved. Name that tune in 50,000 notes and then some. Confetti deaf ears with the tones of who you *are*, of who you *will be*, of who you *will to be*. And, for God's sake, dance, dance, dance.

"YOU CAN'T BUILD A REPUTATION ON
WHAT YOU'RE GOING TO DO."

~HENRY FORD

Follow me, if you so dare, my contemplatively curious *compadres*, into the wondrous world of the future perfect. A lush land where possibilities seem to clutter the ground, like fallen fruit from trees of wisdom and wishes, greatness and grandeur. Regardless of your voluminously varied vital stats, I'm willing to bet you have all frolicked in such a Polaroid place, picturing the gifts that will copiously fill your beseeching baskets. Perhaps early retirement, perfect health, a much-awaited vacation, a gleaming white smile, a fabulous home life, a coveted sense of inner peace, and a good night's sleep. But hey, why stop there? If we're fanning out what *you will have attained...someday*, why not toss in a set of loving in-laws, a dog that won't bite, stress-free Mondays, fewer wrinkles, and that new Lexus? This can all be yours. Someday.

With the naive optimism of a dim-witted child, you've undoubtedly attempted to forecast this future perfect. Didn't quite happen, huh? So what got in the way of the dream life becoming a reality? I'll venture to guess virtual reality slapped you upside the head with a litany of immediate efforts needed to bring such a vision to fruition. You know as well as I, the Wall Street bottom line behind a fabulous future: It ain't yours to *have*, it's yours to *make*, and the making starts today. Today's lesson, then: You can't build your life on what you're *going to do*.

Many of you have unknowingly exemplified this commonsensical truth through and for the survival of your professional life. Am I right? So, let's revisit the plentiful path of your career and review how it unfolded. Through muck and mire, it eventually led you to a land adorned with gifts of success and respect, responsibility, and trust. Perhaps dear Henry's premise of promise has flickered in the background of your professional path of growth, and you've invested wisely, even cornered the market on understanding the necessity of *doing*.

And now, your working harvest bears fruits to feast upon. But what about the other half of your life? What of the daydreams of your *personal* life, of family and friends, love and charity, health and happiness? Are they equally, dutifully fertilized with sacrifice, strategy, and heart-full efforts of *doing*? Have you neglected such diligence to the future perfect of what lies beyond the secured stretch of your business card? Know that all the plans, charts, goals, promises, and resolutions won't bring a smile to your face and aren't worth a dime, if they only fill a journal, cover a chalkboard, or fall upon deaf ears—namely your own. Build a balanced life. Become a whole person. Make your future perfect, today.

"OH, THAT YOU WOULD BLESS ME
INDEED, AND ENLARGE MY TERRITORY,

THAT YOUR HAND WOULD BE WITH ME,
AND THAT YOU WOULD KEEP ME FROM
EVIL"

~I CHRONICLES

38

Honorable guests, the day has arrived,

When mightier meanings osmose.

Trusting to bless with gifts long-lost scribed,

I garnish a prayer of prose.

Believers and doubters abound, all the same,

For I know only where I stand

In giving my thanks, professing each name,

This Prayer of Jabez doth expand.

This selection, offers yet another leap of faith, as I elect to satiate my unyielding capriciousness in candor. Perhaps these words will garner sanctuary, a mantra in the making. Or, perhaps, you've entertained a comparable concoction of words, whose fellowship stirs up effervescent energy and powerful peace. Regardless of the literature, rhetoric, or lyrics, pay mind merely to their beautiful message. Yield to their vitality, go forth and multiply!

"THE PROBLEM IS NEVER HOW TO GET NEW, INNOVATIVE THOUGHTS INTO YOUR MIND, BUT HOW TO GET OLD ONES OUT."

~DEE HOCK

Survey the Nobel Prize-winning theories, Yogi Berra-isms, musings of Lee Iacocca, or hackneyed adages of childhood which lay parked, idle in your frontal lobe, ready at a moment's notice to intellectually integrate your daily activities and paths of thought. An impressive pack of Hummers, their collective underlying message of truth and common sense arms you with fuel to wise up, step up, and take on the world of change. Give 'em some gas and watch 'em go!

Yet, even as the search for fresher ideas to grow bigger-better-faster-wiser has no end, you probably tolerate the garage-full of weathered umpiring and dopey-sounding phrases of profundity that confetti your every conversation. The problem, folks, lies not in the content, the context, nor the delivery. Instead, it's jammed up with the actions you choose to take, or not to take to utilize such eloquence.

Sound about right? Have you got your mind so set in its ways that the tried and true mementos, let alone the cutting-edge concepts, don't have a snowball's chance to make it past your ears and into your brain to elicit a response toward betterment? Is your "system" working for you or against you? Well, I challenge you to do a little house cleaning, so-to-speak, and start with the upstairs. Clear out the cobwebs of your cranium, tune up your worn parts, and fill up with the rocket fuel of nouveau ideas!

"THE MIRACLE, OR THE POWER, THAT ELEVATES THE FEW IS TO BE FOUND IN THEIR PERSEVERANCE UNDER THE PROMPTINGS OF A BRAVE, DETERMINED SPIRIT."

~MARK TWAIN

40

Such enigmatic mutterings of dear Samuel Clemens halo the mind with grand dressage, perhaps worthy only of royalty. Yet, the modern day heroes I behold day upon day have earned equal ownership, righteously upholding regal values and deeds while humbly donning the titles of leader and listener.

I have unyielding faith in each and every one of you that you hold a miracle within, a power that has guided you through the depths of humility, strife, and bureaucratic brew-ha-ha to the blindingly coveted caverns of a life of blessed citizenry. When opportunity has presented itself, undoubtedly you have taken the bull by the horns, slain the dragon of demise, and gotten back up on the bucking horse. You have dug deep enough to release and relish your inner strength, not only to the benefit of yourself, but to that of your very own peanut gallery of family, friends, and fans.

So, how do you keep on keepin' on? Try your damnedest to never forget those defining moments, movements, and missions. Dream about them, story tell them, sprinkle them in your bath, toss 'em into your martini as often as your calendared and categorized brains can schedule it in. In one stroke, these hole-in-one highs can fire up an ignition sequence that no self-help, band-aid therapy book could ever attempt to deliver.

Tap into your brave, determined spirit and spread its snowballing wonder into the crevasses you've forgotten and filed away. When you choose to change your underlying structures of cobwebbed perspective, you set in motion an awesome operation of the natural selection of *self*. The elbow grease gloriously pays off and the roller coaster peaks deliver a ride, all the more inviting, exciting, and self-inspiring.

The spirit of your inner strength, in turn, glows an amber ember, signaling the miracle seed, planted so long ago, to blossom. For even as your body and mind need nourishment to bear harvest, so does your valiant spirit.

41

"We all walk in the dark and each
of us must learn to turn on his or
her own light."

~Earl Nightingale

Houston, we have a problem. But, fear not the profundity. Just as such a statement effortlessly, yet never randomly, rolls off the tongue, I anticipate hands and eyebrows on the rise. And so I scurry to expound, trusting that silent swill of *thank yous* shall erupt when all is said and done.

I take it upon myself to angle the mirror once again for your viewing pleasure, to simply reveal the *you* that your omnipresent audience has the opportunity to experience. With the stage perpetually set, the play is indefinitely scripted. Yet, the irony surfaces in the secret of your character's name, for the role you fill incessantly changes. Each person you create emerges with a new set of rules, expectations, strengths, and behaviors in an unconscious attempt to assimilate to the surrounding people, places, and things.

In each scene you don a different halo, sport a trademarked logo, embroidered for all to lay eyes upon. You are mother, father, sweetheart, sibling, seeker, client, customer, CEO, director, athlete, warden, servant, bad driver, great tipper, starving artist, fabulous friend, pain-in-the-ass neighbor, leader, listener, lover, lifesaver. You've adopted some roles of your own volition. You've acquired others through various means. But in all, your impact is immeasurably significant, albeit invariably undisclosed.

And so I ask, what if you witnessed your nametag change with each passage from meeting time to bonding time? What if you heard the music morph as you transition from deadline to waiting line, from typing emails to tying shoes, from "Who are you?" to "I love you"?

What if you bolstered the caliber of involvement in your characters' developments and consciously absorbed your free-flowing, altering behaviors? Perhaps the aphoristic lesson lies in stepping out of your own shoes, exiting stage left, and joining the ubiquitous crowd, to extract the essence of each rotated role.

Import a sense of appreciation uniquely inherent to the mosaic myriad of tattoos predicated not by you, but by the theater surrounding you. Torch the stage lights to unveil the truth floating beneath the under-conversation of your *self*. For we share one common irony woven throughout our collective *Truman Show*: We all play the lead, my friends.

"THE ONE IMPORTANT THING I HAVE LEARNED OVER THE YEARS IS THE DIFFERENCE BETWEEN TAKING ONE'S WORK SERIOUSLY AND TAKING ONE'S SELF SERIOUSLY. THE FIRST IS IMPERATIVE AND THE SECOND IS DISASTROUS."

~DAME MARGOT FONTEYN

Some people are blessed to have found their true calling, or passion, at a relatively young age, and they exude the delight of their discovery. But they also make no bones about the fact that they're strapped in for the long haul and have another 30, 40, 50 years to hone their craft, attain great strides, make many mistakes, take even more risks, and hopefully have a recognizable impact on the world, as they fit into it. Rarely do they express fear of the misfortunes, errors, or antagonists that will attempt to humble them along their path to personal greatness and fulfillment. And oftentimes their sense of humor and humility is their saving grace.

But, what's that, you say? What about those of us who haven't found "it" just yet? Here's a little help. Imagine unplugging yourself from those activities, events, and relationships within your profession that spark your verve for life, reminding you of *why* you do *what* you do to make a life while making a living. Fifty bucks says it's *those very things* that keep you from taking your role all too seriously, and none of them are a waste of time.

A paycheck is a paycheck and we all put our pants on the same way. But life is too short and potentially too sweet to treat it like another project, client, case study, or moneymaking business plan. If you're still looking to define that passion in your daily life, maybe it's right in front of you. You just need to open your eyes, loosen up, and remember that this ain't a dress rehearsal! It's okay to act a fool. You're really just being human.

43

I've got a question for you: What's the value of that Real Estate between your ears? No doubt, it sits at prime rate, a prominent investment for any capitalist these days. Yet what a shame if you never hold an open house to showcase the lavish landscape, intricate architecture, and fabulous collectibles on which you have stamped your name and appreciated its value.

And so, my fellow walking books of knowledge, what is on your agenda of action today? What's been brewing, stewing, and spewing from mind to mouth that you need to act upon? *Is today the day* you dig into the neglected nest of nimbleness and grease your elbows? Will you march forward with workmanship, manuscript, or sacrifice? Perhaps, walk the talk and jump off the fixed fence of fluctuation?

I say, *make today the day*. Take flight. Move and shake with the best of 'em, and don't worry about explanations, manifestations, or configurations. With brain brimmed and blueprints inked, exercise a path of exposition, exploration, and execution. Make, move, groove, do, wave, riddle, and beat. Today.

"I BELIEVE THAT UNARMED TRUTH AND UNCONDITIONAL LOVE WILL HAVE THE FINAL WORD IN REALITY."

~DR. MARTIN LUTHER KING, JR.

44

Friends, Romans, countrymen, although the King's words seemingly resonate the paint-by-number simplicity of an idealist's palate, I see no harm in letting the mind follow a longing heart. But have you a stockpile of stoic fundamentals to which you flock: A smattering of should's and shouldn'ts, do's and don'ts, and revered, yet vagrant values, once pure, now petrified? Ever considered digging around a bit to unveil what may be absent, overlooked, or obliviously neglected? Well, then, I suggest an excavation.

Join me in yet another earthly dissection of that which we build our glass houses around and upon. Join me in an elective root canal of the self. And what better time to granulate the ground upon which we walk, when spring has sprung? Rumor has it, 'tis the season for love in the air, but what about the other months? Is the L-word reserved for sprouting blossoms and teenagers? Is the truth of who you are and what beats your very heart a stranger in your own reality?

Look beyond the aromatic allergens and belligerent bugs filling the air and note what rises above the buzz, the boss, and the BS. Trench away more filler and see what's fixin' to sprout beneath the pettiness, pit bulls, and pinheads. *C'est l'amour*, folks!

But, have you back-burnered and reserved love for just those people and things in your life that gratify, satisfy, and return the same percentage? Who, what, when, where, why, and how do you love?

When all is said and done, love is the one truth that offers security, sanctuary, salvation, and sanity to any and all who recognize the solution in its wondrous reach. It fills and fulfills, unleashes and unloads, colors and creates, blooms and blesses all who embrace its essence.

So I say, dig it up and set it free from the swaddling, suffocating weeds. Think about it, build on it, nestle in it, and resonate with it. Plant it, share it, spread it, instigate it, and integrate it. Love.

"Wisdom is the reward you get for a lifetime of listening when you would rather have talked."

~Mark Twain

Hey, I've got something to say, world!

Ever find yourself struggling simply to get a word in edge-wise, let alone take in what others spew, shout, and spoon-feed you? Perhaps this parade and tirade of intrusive, incessant babbling, which fills the air, your space, and your noggin, forces you to belligerently banter above the minutia! Oh, the *noise, noise, noise*!

Now, I refuse to sport the title of Grinch, but fifty bucks says I'm not the only one out there struggling to hear myself think. Oftentimes it seems that we shuttle from conversation to conversation, volleying from dialog to monologue, leaping from one soapbox to another, hell-bent on being heard and acknowledged. After all, only the bold survive, right?

Yet, as hindsight readily delivers the best lessons learned, albeit to a fault, perhaps there's a best-kept secret in foresight, shifting the playing field in the favor of wallflowers versus wind-up toys. Enter Twain and his simple suggestive message: What's the shouting all about?

What did you miss while defending yourself, driving home a point, explaining the details, clearing the room, or getting your two cents in? Step back and fancy what happens when you quietly curtail the questioning and commenting, lull the laughing and tomfoolery, and settle the grunting and grumbling. Tune in to the walking books of knowledge, the bearers of eye-opening epiphanies, and the significant silences whispering the fruits of wisdom. Jump aboard this learning curve ride to enlightenment, growth, and peace of mind. But keep quiet!

"EVERY EXIT IS AN ENTRY SOMEWHERE ELSE."

~TOM STOPPARD

46

Ahhhhh….umphhh! Sound familiar? These are the welcoming sounds of yet another graceful landing into the minutia of a Monday morning. Some, certainly, a bit more humbling than others, like those who curtail the joy of a well-deserved vacation. Reappearing by your bedside like a neighbor's kid that just won't leave; ruthlessly shunting your arm with an invisible IV of flurry, scurry, and worry. Coming off a junket's high of enchantment-filled city lights or shooting stars and country air, you can't help but think of the peacefulness, simplicity, and lack of an agenda that lovingly distracted you for a few days away from home base.

Somehow you freed your pea-pod brain from the guilt of obligation and exited stage left to the behind-the-scenes world of nothing to do, nowhere to go, and no hurry to finish. And you always seem to find yourself asking,"Why did I wait so long to do this?"

Funny how we psyche ourselves up for time off from the everyday brew-ha-ha. Invariably we spotlight that which we *will not* miss, *will not* bring with us, will (hopefully) not worry about. Some of us probably even jot down a "Not to Do" list. Regardless of the measures or antics, our lack of a game plan allows us to perhaps purr a few more catnaps or capture a few minutes of meditation, dive into a good read, a long walk, or uninterrupted bath. Ironically, though, as we purposefully escape the drama and burnout of stress, we randomly traipse into the embrace of an abyss. And that, my friends, is a beautiful thing.

Folks, that catnap holds more value than all the Serta stock in the world. Likewise, that book and bath will take you to a place your noggin has probably never been or barely remembers. That walk sans pedometer, parameters, or pace-markers could prove the best damn cardio-salsa your heart has ever endured!! Whether you leave the clamp of corporate culture for three days or three minutes, recognize that the element of time is not the defining variable, the *leaving* is. Trust that this transient movement from people, places, and things simply clears the path to new ideas, new experiences, and new entries into a place with your name over the door.

89

"THE BASIC DIFFERENCE BETWEEN AN
ORDINARY MAN AND A WARRIOR IS THAT
THE WARRIOR TAKES EVERYTHING AS A
CHALLENGE, WHILE AN ORDINARY MAN
TAKES EVERYTHING AS A BLESSING OR
A CURSE."

~CARLOS CASTENEDA

Ante up, folks.

Think critically about what's clouding your rose-colored 20/20 perspective or, worse yet, producing an irrevocable hiccup in your hopeful path of least resistance. Is someone causing you to harbor a Louis Vuitton overnight bag of resentment? Has difficulty accessorized your ensemble with a proverbial monkey on your back? Have you hit a wall? Are you moldering over writer's block? Dealing with disappointment? Grieving a loss? Groaning about a broken nail, broken heart, or broken life? Well, hang in there.

I, too, have been there, done that. I don't want to pour salt on your wounds, nor will I face-jam you with June Cleaver clichés and tell you to take a physic. Instead, I've paged this litany of difficulties because I propose that the gravity of each example perhaps warrants the same marquis space for contemplation. Since we can rarely choose our battles, let alone the outcomes, the impact each of these obstacles has upon us varies from person to person. It's all relative. Therein, I believe, lies the resounding, irrefutable *a-ha*!

Success in the face of diversity becomes a metaphoric picture of hanging on while others let go. Think you're doomed, and you are. Think you're Superman, and you'll find yourself flying high with cape flailing.

Do you believe all gifts beam down from Heaven and all tragedies boil up from Hell? As we force ourselves to get granular, we may find the root shooting bloom to these diametrically opposing beliefs. Truth unveiled, the difficulty lies not in the breadth of the challenge but in your mind and heart. Will you fold if no Aces fill your hand today, even if the whole deck holds not-a-one? Or, will you choose to exult in the battle of learning, the dance of loving, the lament in losing, and the joy of living? After all, your perspective is your reality…and there's nothing ordinary about that.

48

"EVERYTHING HAPPENS FOR A REASON."

~SOME FOOL

Trust me, folks, I, too, wish I had a dime for every bloody time someone offered me this tattered security blanket as solace for the hard-knock that I may have just weathered. But, you and I both know that statements like this, glowing with good ol' common sense, really need neither decoration nor drum-roll, for they are timeless golden nuggets of wisdom.

Suffice it to say, I have not reached the bottom of the barrel of witticism and wonderment, nor am I scheming to pass this antiquated morsel off as new and improved. Yea, I shall go forth and soapbox, in a humble attempt to peel back the layers and reveal a fresh, yet spicy new recipe for your dining pleasure.

"Everything happens for a reason." Damn, there it is again! True, this timeless canonical philosophy may offer comfort and peace, albeit temporal. However, it alludes to the mystery of the event's occurrence in the first place. And under furrowed brow, through squinted orbs, we assign ourselves to the quest of acquiring the very reason for the

thing that happened. Perhaps we pray that retrospective contemplation will birth an acceptable answer. Alas, we still sit with the restlessness that the environs of the world around us hold the reins and lead us through sunshine and hail, leaving us only to react or respond accordingly.

With hand feebly raised, then, I voice the following request: Entertain the equally commonsensical, yet introspective premise *"Every<u>one</u> happens for a reason."* Reconnect the former unsatisfying, dangling ellipsis to this refreshing tangibility of your *self*. Humor me, and turn the tables on your very own situations, travesty, and comedy alike.

Stop pondering the incessant *why* of the plethora of phenomena swilling around you. Instead, plant the seed: *Everyone*, indeed, happens for a reason, and begin to nourish it with thoughts and energies that put you back at the head of the table. Embrace the perspective that you have charge of the landscape from which you emerge, and perhaps the hackneyed yet seemingly out-of-reach right place, right time scenario is closer than you think.

So, go on and happen! Branch out. Build a reason for your grand existence. Create a work of art for the gods. Confetti the world with your *why*. Make waves. Make mistakes. Make noise. Hell, make a mess, all in the knowing that though the weeds may sprout, you shall still have your rose bushes.

"In the middle of difficulty, lies opportunity."

~Albert Einstein

49

Well now, that's a surprise, huh? How many times has something gone to hell-in-a-hand-basket only to miraculously return with gifts and glory. Invariably the blessing in disguise presents itself as merely the parting gift, only to yield fruits, perchance, beyond our imagination's grasp. If only our short-term memories could press the replay button from the myriad moments past, where, from the relentless tugs-of-war, we emerged from the trenches triumphant. If only the intrinsic resilience in our spirits would shake some sense into our fear-triggered security system, it might settle our high-alert nerves. For, with that reminiscent reassurance, we might see through the entangling weeds of challenge to the amazing blooms that have duly erupted, time and time again.

Needless to say, you know what *difficulty* looks like. You've survived it, swallowed it, sweated it out, and stared it down, no doubt with knees knocking. Yet, how do you define *opportunity* and how do you recognize it when it comes knocking? If you expect it to excitedly rush up to you, dressed to the nines, donning a crown—you've got a long wait. So pack a lunch. Maybe, secretly, you hope it looks like a winning lottery ticket, a fluke purchase gone incredibly well!

In either case, you're on the lookout for it. On the other hand, some of you may meekly fixate on the four surrounding walls of your existence, so that opportunity couldn't present itself even if it could scale your fortress.

> "Mᴀɴʏ ᴏꜰ ᴜꜱ ʜᴀᴠᴇ ʜᴇᴀʀᴅ ᴏᴘᴘᴏʀᴛᴜɴɪᴛʏ ᴋɴᴏᴄᴋɪɴɢ ᴀᴛ ᴏᴜʀ ᴅᴏᴏʀ, ʙᴜᴛ ʙʏ ᴛʜᴇ ᴛɪᴍᴇ ᴡᴇ ᴜɴʜᴏᴏᴋᴇᴅ ᴛʜᴇ ᴄʜᴀɪɴ, ᴘᴜꜱʜᴇᴅ ʙᴀᴄᴋ ᴛʜᴇ ʙᴏʟᴛ, ᴛᴜʀɴᴇᴅ ᴛᴡᴏ ʟᴏᴄᴋꜱ, ᴀɴᴅ ꜱʜᴜᴛ ᴏꜰꜰ ᴛʜᴇ ʙᴜʀɢʟᴀʀ ᴀʟᴀʀᴍ—ɪᴛ ᴡᴀꜱ ɢᴏɴᴇ!"
>
> ~Aɴᴏɴʏᴍᴏᴜꜱ

You and I both know that all the preparation and expectation in the world won't prime you for what is *inside* that glorious package labeled *A Fabulous Opportunity for You*. What's more, the surprise will lie equally in the wrapping and delivery, perhaps disheveled or dazzling, poured on or propped up, random pieces or Rembrandts. All the same, each and every one comes addressed to you and will fit you like a glove.

"POWERFUL LEADERS ARE PERPETUAL LEARNERS."

~HOWARD HENDRICKS & MEL CURE

Humor me, folks, and take a trip down the path of humility-rich, character-building flashbacks of days gone by. Allow yourself to traipse through the vivid snapshots of countless times your age-defining inexperience caught you in the headlights. When once upon-a-time, a simple knee-jerk shrug of your naive shoulders was all you knew to offer and undeniably fit the bill without further expounding necessary. Better yet, bask in the effervescent glee whence, "I don't know," was an absolute, self-appeasing response to the barrage of authority-dealt inquiries.

Ahhh...bashful, yet blissful ignorance, a perfect excuse for past-tensed stutterings, embarrassing moments, and conversation black holes. Blessed were such times, which laid the mosaic groundwork for future experience, extraction, education, and excellence. We tight-roped the cusp of force-fed literature and lessons, arithmetic and advice, technology and trivia. We sought answers from both literal and metaphorical books of knowledge and lapped up information with thirst-quenching excitement. Remember those days?

Take heed, for as we segue out of the open range of unaccountable adolescence, we stumble into the mystically mapped, obstacle-laden trails of adulthood. Here the inhabitants javelin expectations and judgments our way, often damaging our innocence and creating fear in our once secure sense of survival. Still, the beautiful landscape may offer fabulous fruits of redeeming experience, but too often we scurry back to our barricaded home base, flip on the neon "I don't care" sign, and unwittingly resort to a stifling existence of independence.

So the truth comes out! And it sounds like a bad case of *pride*. The four-letter-word with an extra letter attitude that will forever forest-over your eyes and ears, losing you in the labyrinth of a discontented life. She carries great destruction, limiting joy, stirring up conflict, and dividing people from paved paths of fellowship. She is, perhaps, the mother of all vices. But where there's a will, there's a way to weave your life in opposition of her evil lure.

Begin by owning up to your mistakes, for they are garnished with invaluable lessons. Elect to follow your own pointed suggestions and set the example without laying claim to the fabulously shining crown that accompanies such a pedestal. Honor your intrinsic need for help and embrace the power behind asking for it! In turn, your spirited sphere of influence will choose to rush the runway to you in service and support. Bottom line: Learn to love to learn and the leadership will follow.

"HOPE SPRINGS ETERNAL IN THE HUMAN
BREAST; MAN NEVER IS, BUT ALWAYS
TO BE BLEST. THE SOUL, UNEASY AND
CONFIN'D FROM HOME, RESTS AND
EXPATIATES IN A LIFE TO COME."

~ALEXANDER POPE

Alas, I cannot compete with such elite profundity. Still, I poise my simple prose to linger and move you to and through grand tides.

Cautious he once stood, indeed in kind

Slow of heart, simple of mind.

His distorted view net fearsome lasting

Insatiable wondering if hope bore casting.

Cautious wishing of if-and-when

He prayed be proven right...yea, if-and-then.

A choice now plated to ebb, fail and fall,

Or measure be slated to rise wherewithal.

Strong now in spirit, indeed in kind

Confidence confirmed, in heart, in mind.

He stands in truth to fight the good fight

Illuminated with hope and belief charged bright.

Strong conceiving of blind faith ne'er waning

His hope sprung eternal yields gifts worth waiting.

~Kimberlie Dykeman

And so, a story about *he*—perhaps *you*, *me*, and *they* as well—wherein lies discovery of the err of unfounded, undefined wishing. But wait! *He* emerges triumphant with understanding and resilience; for *having faith* fills his sights to fruitful embrace. Question is, what story writes your life? Do you entrust hope in tomorrow's blessings, or do you merely pray the day arrives?

"I HOPE I MAY NEVER BE GUILTY OF
WRITING ANYTHING INTENDED TO MAKE
POOR PEOPLE CONTENTED WITH THEIR
LOT. I WOULD RATHER BE KNOWN AS ONE
WHO SOUGHT TO INSPIRE HIS READERS
WITH A DIVINE DISCONTENT. TO MAKE
MEN AND WOMEN DISCONTENTED WITH
BAD HEALTH, AND TO SHOW THEM HOW,
BY HARD WORK, THEY CAN HAVE BETTER
HEALTH. TO MAKE THEM DISCONTENTED
WITH THEIR INTELLIGENCE, AND TO
STIMULATE THEM TO CONTINUED STUDY.
TO URGE THEM ON TO BETTER JOBS,
BETTER HOMES, MORE MONEY IN THE
BANK. BUT IT DOES NOT HARM, IN OUR
STRIVING AFTER THESE WORTH-WHILE
THINGS, TO PAUSE ONCE IN A WHILE
AND COUNT OUR BLESSINGS."

~BRUCE BARTON

One could get lost in these words, hoping that within our labyrinth of jigsaw-puzzled days, we have the opportunity to follow such wishful thinkings, or perchance we already watermark these values on our collective loyal peanut gallery of fans, friends, and families.

This tremendous, all-encompassing delivery of perspective and motivation, serves to prime the wheels to move yet again in a forward, freeing motion for the betterment of present and future. Swaddle yourself in the message of working smarter, feeling stronger, looking better, and living longer, all the while striving for diligence in toil, battling for true cause, and glorifying the high bar of excellence.

Hang on for a second, though, because Barton's back-door face-jam of pending obligation will catch you right in the kisser and, with a swift kick in the pants, reveals to you a moral, societal insistence in sharing the wealth. Now, drum up a memory of days gone by, wherein you eyeballed your mirrored self as porter of titles, utterly countless, yet collectively priceless, and viewed your span of influence and impression with beautiful blind omnipotence. Saturate your linear-thinking self with the possibility of a portfolio of growing greatness, empirically showering neighbor and stranger alike. Push, drive, provoke, egg on, and eek out the power of others to never find fashion in the four corners of a box. And as givers gain, therein lies myriad blessings.

"HAPPINESS IS A BUTTERFLY WHICH,
WHEN PURSUED IS ALWAYS BEYOND
OUR GRASP, BUT WHICH, IF YOU WILL
SIT DOWN QUIETLY, MAY ALIGHT UPON
YOU."

~NATHANIEL HAWTHORNE

53

Sit still!

No, I'm not scolding you. I'm saving you from stripping your gears and burning out your engine! Pop a squat in the passenger's seat of your very own merry-go-round of minutia and note the passing possibilities, pleasure, and peace. Tough to do, huh? Well, no wonder. Thoughtlessly tossing yield signs to the wind, many of us careen ignorantly through our numbered days, driving into a reckless state of mayhem. Restlessly wondering where time has flown, our hot pursuit of healthy, wealthy, wise, and happy ironically becomes but a spec in the rear-view mirror.

Foolishly, our MapQuested minds seek a AAA discount when fast-forwarding through life's TripTik, yet we righteously find fault with our speedway world. In truth, our collective feet on the gas pedal prove that *bigger-better-faster* ain't all it's cracked up to be when the finish line stands empty.

Shhh! Again, dump the knee-jerk negative connotation of childhood discipline and trust that this, too, is for your own good. Bite your tongue and hear how your discourse has diminished into two-bit, misfit mutterings, holding little meat, and even less meaning. Fifty bucks says you can count on one hand the number of fabulously fulfilling conversations parked on your past-tensed palate, not to mention the back-seat-driver dialog between you and yourself. Remember the joy in verbose heart-to-hearts? And, when was the last time you enlightened your noggin sans critique and corruption? Why not silence the mechanical whir and blur and play back the tracks to unveil the irresponsible party?

Fearlessly trust that the experiences in your life's daily journey sparkle through every relationship, first founded then sustained through the mighty spoken word. Assign significance to these exchanges and they will mean all the more at the next fuel-up. Choose to dissolve yourself in the priceless sanctuary of unstructured timelessness and yield to uncalculated quiet. Absorb the beauty in the tour knowing that the flow of life's traffic will move you without burying the needle. For the driver's seat will remain calmly at your command, but the ride will leave you joyous and effortlessly breathless.

"BEING DEFEATED IS OFTEN A TEMPORARY CONDITION. GIVING UP IS WHAT MAKES IT PERMANENT."

~MARILYN VOS SAVANT

54

Join me for a moment and sift through the facts and feelings of a collective defining moment that united the ends of the earth in the blink of an eye.

They, the omnipotent and seemingly omniscient minds of the world, say the older we get, the faster time seems to fly. Without warning, another year passes, again commemorating September 11th's infamous global wake-up call that yanked us from the high-tech trance of our golden monitors. Another 365 feeble days later and lifetimes wiser, we face the anniversaries of 9-11, perhaps with breath held and fear revisiting, or perhaps with little more than a moment of silence.

Regardless of temporal recognition or reaction, we hear no placating John Lennon tune filling the airwaves, challenging us to visualize a seamless sanctuary, no Willie Nelson Fest to reconnect us as people of the land. Instead, each of us alone will decide how to engrave this day into our very beings. Perhaps a mere continuation of struggle, long-awaited closure yielding clarity, or a true celebration of the life, liberty, and pursuit of happiness we still have the luxury of leading.

Now consider yourself. Do you still rummage through the smoldering ruins of 2001, let alone the calamities of other years? Do you still attempt to make sense of your own Ground Zero? Regardless of its relative gravity, first impact of any great gloom forces the natural selection of self and survival to kick in, but fifty bucks says the barrage of after-effects settles you into a safe, yet suffocating domain of eggshells and excuses.

In the grayness of a stagnant middle management of your own life, you might stand over-stuffed with ideas you can't propose without consent, over-shadowed by issues you can't solve without support. Physically and financially, socially and psychologically, your personal balance sheet may appear its very own WTC. And yet, life springs from beneath the rubble.

Take it from a man who never threw in the towel. General Douglas MacArthur affirmed, "There is no security on this earth; there is only opportunity."

Perhaps some such tragedy offered a first time to rebuild from the ground-up. Oftentimes you do it better the second time around. But as fluffed and floral as that may sound, it comes accompanied by a grave caveat to self-destruction:

Be ginger with the nightcaps of nostalgia, for reflection without resolution will only keep the record skipping.

And so, my friends, ponder the thought that you may very well sit better off, having stood at attention during this time. With an enlivened perspective of the here and now, an appreciation of interdependence, and a gamut of clear choices to re-boot a once-collapsed tower of achievements, you need only put one foot in front of the other. Build a trust in both yourself and the world that surrounds, acknowledging that the media fat pipe can only report in the past tense. Choose to create your own headlines and fill the pages with the glorious future only you can believe into being.

"COURAGE IS NOT THE ABSENCE OF FEAR, BUT RATHER THE JUDGMENT THAT SOMETHING ELSE IS MORE IMPORTANT THAN FEAR."

~AMBROSE REDMOON

55

The operative notion here is a four-letter word named *Fear*—that universal imp that can wheedle its way into the hearts of tycoon and street urchin alike. Undoubtedly, it has devilishly danced on shoulders and nestled pillows and furtively frolicked in boardroom and bedroom without fatigue. It sits at attention with laptop at arms, tapping abundance to the list of terrors and trepidations.

Certainly the immeasurable frights of worldly plight are mere blips on our collective radar screens. We halt for a moment in an attempt to comprehend the awesome dilemmas, yet our noggins have little space for the woes of the world. Instead we find ourselves mesmerized and manipulated by the effervescent horrors that chase us.

What do you fear? What invariably tattoos the deer-in-the-headlights look upon your brow? What scares the bejeezus out of you day or night? Death? Age? Marriage? Divorce? Love? Taxes? Unemployment? Uncle Sam? Silence? God? The Boogie Man? Solitude? Public speaking? Kids? No money? Failure? War? Not being happy? Not making a difference? Never becoming famous? Never finding true love?

Born out of ignorance or avoidance, maybe even genetic disposition, it breathes and breeds. And try as you diligently may to avoid its arrival in your filing-system's frontal lobe, fear still creeps in like funk.

It clenches you when you know there are great things at stake, great memories being made, great people sharing the fruits of your life. Oh, but circumstance offers but one determinant of how inflated any imminence of danger will grow. Luckily the size of the battle within you has the power to belittle these assumed omnipotent challenges. Trust in the idea that you have the intrinsic ability to diminish the battalion of dreads and demons, equipping you to see the forest *and* the trees, and protect that which makes your life what you desire. You need only feed and fuel that morsel of bravery to bore through and stand triumphant with love and loyalty, faith and fervor. So go forth with courage in heart, mind, and spirit and light a cigar in celebration.

"THE BEST THING ABOUT THE FUTURE IS THAT IT COMES ONLY ONE DAY AT A TIME."

~ABRAHAM LINCOLN

56

Makes sense, right? Though many will yield to the path of preemie pomp and submit to the barrage of daily, let alone monthly pre-game pressure. My suggestion? Heed a bit of Abe's advice and choose to follow the yellow brick road as it reveals itself in smoothly satiating, calendared steps. Sure, either route begins and ends on the same spot in time, but the wise shopper acknowledges that his little cart can only carry one Dolce & Gabbana day at a time.

thanks·giv·ing (thăngks-gĭv´ĭng) N. AN ACT OF GIVING THANKS; AN EXPRESSION OF GRATITUDE

57

Hope you're hungry, because this timely concoction of culinary soapboxing doles out not one, but two servings of epicurean delight to drive home a notion that so very many of us have overlooked, and continue to pass over.

In black and white, the operative word here is *giving*. Needless to say, the actual form of the *thanks* takes on as much importance as the act itself. Some slaps on the back are best soft-served with a smile. Still, this world-renowned date for thanks-giving has been anchored in time by our forefathers in an unyielding attempt to showcase its kinetic nature. And so, I ask that you humor me with this two-for-one homage to the aromatic brilliance of a few of connoisseurs of the Canon.

1st Course

> "LET US REMEMBER THAT, AS MUCH HAS BEEN GIVEN US, MUCH WILL BE EXPECTED FROM US, AND THAT TRUE HOMAGE COMES FROM THE HEART AS WELL AS FROM THE LIPS, AND SHOWS ITSELF IN DEEDS."
>
> ~THEODORE ROOSEVELT

You are the main ingredient and you're alive and kicking! You may even have all your fingers and toes, as well as a college education, and the luxury of pushing pause to digest this meal of literary morsels. Burrow in and bear-hug the irrefutable fact that you are truly blessed, and, in turn, equally limitless in opportunities to show appreciation for the gifts you've received.

2nd Course

> "AS WE EXPRESS OUR GRATITUDE, WE MUST NEVER FORGET THAT THE HIGHEST APPRECIATION IS NOT TO UTTER WORDS, BUT TO LIVE BY THEM."
>
> ~JOHN FITZGERALD KENNEDY

Go ahead and dish 'em out however you choose, stuffed between hors d'oeuvres or piled high atop Mom's fabulous pecan pie. Fifty bucks says your belly-full sensation of satisfaction comes not from the feast of fruitcake, but from your dynamic expression of thanks for the boundless bounties before you. Fill your Tupperware with these leftovers—and season the rest of your days with provisions that'll never spoil—regardless of the cook!

58

"LIFE BEGINS AT THE END OF YOUR COMFORT ZONE."

~N.D.WALSCH

I don't know about you, but if this premise rings true, then many of you can identify a year, let alone an era, in which you have *truly* lived. Proudly acknowledge that you have also strived and survived the confounded labyrinth of potholes and prop doors. And with mosaic-ed prayer and possibility in hand, you have deciphered the hieroglyphics to unfold an irrefutably timeless and timely fact: *Training wheels are meant to be taken off.*

So, as I take my place at the helm of this little soapbox, I say, "Comfort, shmomfort." Roll up your sleeves, toss on a helmet, kick up the stand, and pop a wheelie down the open road of adventure. Start each blessed year with the wind in your face and your hair on fire and see where the journey takes you!

"PATIENCE AND PERSEVERANCE HAVE A MAGICAL EFFECT BEFORE WHICH DIFFICULTIES DISAPPEAR AND OBSTACLES VANISH."

~JOHN QUINCY ADAMS

Gooooooood morning, race fans! How's the ride so far? Let me guess. As soon as the second hand strikes and Times Square chimes in a clean slate, you set to full throttle and take off like a mid-life-crisis man in a new Corvette.

With heart pounding and champagne in your eyes, you decide that *you will* take the wheel and make things go your way this year, come hell or high water. Righting the wrongs. Shaking the systems. Cutting the fat. Testing the waters. Revolutionizing the resolutions. Painting a free-wheeling, forward thinking phantasmagoric mural of all that is, was, and ever will be the real future perfect you deserve. All in the name of an unyielding loyalty to the natural selection of self, at least until about mid-February.

I must confess, I, too, burn a rouge of rubber just as eagerly each year. Even ponder the thought that the heavens will magically open up and confetti my little field of dreams with all the blessing and adornments that I've kept cooped up for the past twelve months. Sound familiar? Well, I have both good and bad news for you.

Bad news first: A supercharged vehicle won't get you through the roadblocks any faster. No matter how much shifting and strategizing you perform, the course will dictate your life's journey. Not the other way around. And if you're thinking you can brainstorm your agenda-ed TripTik into an immediate reality, think again. Enough with the red line, race fans, you're libel to blow the whole engine again.

Now for the good news: You've already done the work. You've got the ride, the route, and reason for success in all pillars of your future. So, recline with the resonating truth that patience remains the worthwhile virtue that will never fail to fuel your expedition. Coast over your holographic horizon to discover another bountifully balanced year ahead, in body, mind, and spirit. And embrace the magical open road.

Go ahead. No one's looking, and no one's listening either. Take a moment to silence the unfiltered lattice of voices, vehicles, and vultures that whir and stir about on your perpetual passage. Boldly accept this invitation to butterfly an intangible in all its vastness, for the humble hope of simple revelation!

And so I say, *"Knock on the sky..."*

Purposefully prick your ears to the worldly score that backdrops your every sense and stimulation, every walk and wisdom, every commute and coffee talk! Regardless of each moment's holdings, an under-conversation of your ego dials in with a contiguous hum, simultaneously fed by and fueling your thoughts, emotions, and attitude. If you think you can outrun, outwit, or outspin it, think again. It's around you because it *is* you.

"..and listen to the sound."

You alone can identify its resonance. Does it static your ears with speculation, sarcasm, and cynicism? Cry, rattle, and racket; pandemonium and percussion? Trust that this noise of negativity will breed fear and futility as it furrows your brow and postures your body with rigidity and angst. Let the record spin on, and you yourself perpetuate these scratches of anger and arrogance, avoidance and ultimatums, sadness and indifference. Alas, you alone can choose confounded crescendo or glorious harmony.

Just as this smog dews your eardrum with grime, plenty of other stations trumpet possibility and joy, truth and freedom. Preaching humor and harp, jingle and swing. These, my friends, are the vibrations of construction and salvation that will confetti your very being with hope and opportunity as they glean your expressions and pace your body with fluidity and beauty. Choose to speed dial these headquarters of harmonics and you'll unleash the music of grace and groove...even if you ain't got a lick of rhythm in you!

The soundtrack of your life has but one remote control, and you are the sole Mix-master. Embrace the experience of this grand concept and spin it good!

"THE WORLD IS FULL OF ABUNDANCE AND OPPORTUNITY, BUT FAR TOO MANY PEOPLE COME TO THE FOUNTAIN OF LIFE WITH A SIEVE INSTEAD OF A TANK CAR... A TEASPOON INSTEAD OF A STEAM SHOVEL. THEY EXPECT LITTLE AND AS A RESULT THEY GET LITTLE."

~SUCCESS MOTIVATION INSTITUTE

"I can't do that."

"I don't know how."

"I don't have time."

"I won't know anyone."

"I don't know how to get there."

Ugh! Can't you just hear the wasted whining and empty expectations in these excuses? Needless to say, these maladies weed their way into our everyday dialog; seeded in both spoken and unspoken word, contaminating both present and future. So many of us unknowingly dog leash ourselves to our homes, or worse yet, our work, wearing a path of *least existence* and breeding banality, boredom, and bleary sights. Convenience and cruise control become our blinding curse and we no longer even tug the links to see how much slack will yield to our curiosities.

We endlessly commute to and fro with an empty lunch box. We make space for mediocrity and its crumbs. And in a knee-jerk response, we build our own roadblocks, burn our winning lottery tickets, and order the same dry toast, burnt, with a side of soggy bacon.

News flash! The fruit and fruition of life does not begin at your driveway and end at the office door. So, tell me. Why do you expect so little and settle for less? Do you fear revisiting that time in your life when you thought you had the entire world in the palm of your hands? Have you sedated a ravishing hunger to lay your claim on experience and exuberance simply because you're older and presumably wiser? Certainly the landscape has survived a good trouncing, but if you believe that it can still nourish beauty and bounty, it *will*. Your favorite uncle is offering you $100 for being a good kid. Don't tell him you only expected a buck!

Breakout the fine china and large utensils and go back for seconds, even thirds. Make room for a landslide of prosperity. Get a bigger address book. Add on another garage. Forget the inch. Take the mile! Sing for more! Re-sell yourself on the idea that you do indeed have places to go, people to see, and things to do! Retire your micromanaged map of memorized side streets and u-turn onto the open road with globe in hand, a full tank of gas, and an empty flatbed!

"I'M NOT OLD ENOUGH TO KNOW EVERYTHING."

~J.M. BARRIE

Oh, the woes of weathering life, refinancing and reunions, laugh lines and love handles, the proverbial older dogs learning new tricks. At some blessed point, we nod and bow our humbled heads to the undeniable truth: We are no longer the omniscient, ageless sprites we once comic-stripped ourselves to be to infinity and beyond! Ah, well, c'est la vie. Or is it?

In our youth, we naively spent years fighting off the nature of our surroundings—the cynically personified environs that seemed hell-bent on trying, tricking, and taming us into conservative squares of Mary Sunshine and Ward Cleaver. We obtusely parried the droning preachings of law and order, fair and square, perhaps even, stupid is as stupid does, maintaining that we stood everlastingly *in the know*. And, with ego in tow, assumed ourselves leagues smarter than the average bear, let alone Mom, Dad, and every other authority figure.

Then, something changed our collective perspectives, our psychological and physiological make-up; perhaps college graduation, joining the 20+10 club, the event of a first divorce—jeez, maybe even a really good black and white film. Whichever the case, the episodic character-building prompted us to choose truth, love, and interdependence over falsity, indifference, and absolute independence. We experienced a gravitational pull towards doing the right thing, making someone proud, our family, friends, God, even ourselves. And we watched our pockets fill with tangible nuggets of wisdom, albeit deceivingly misshapen and discolored. Regardless of the catalyst though, under further investigation, we see that this coinciding juncture s-p-r-i-n-g-b-o-a-r-d-e-d us into a new realm of thought and a future-perfect of cumulative *a-ha's*.

Oh, but now we spend our entire adulthood perplexed by the complexity of the unsaleable, priceless plot of Real Estate between our two ears. We muse and amuse ourselves simply attempting to decipher the *who, what, where, when, why,* and *how* of our very being! To the point of confounded fatigue, we now fight off the nature in ourselves, insisting we still have so very much to learn. *Forget the rest of the world; I'm still trying to figure out how the heck I got past the third grade!*

But, it doesn't have to be a battle! Throw down your arms and quit dueling with yourself. Purposefully pivot at a bread-crumbed point in your rich past and divert your glazed gaze back to your pockets, now over-filled with rugged nondescript nuggets. Dust off the lint and the cluster shines its amber ember, revealing coveted insight. Look closer, for the wisdom revealed in sheer beauty of perspective eclipses your current discontentment. Trust that this invaluable depth perception has stabilized you through difficult times, people, places, and things. Trust that this ability to see into circumstance has prevented fruitless searches and furnished the sketches of a veritable map toward bountiful outcomes. Finally, cape yourself in this cornucopia of gems of understanding that has gilded you with a gift to confetti truth, love, and interdependence for your entire lifetime.

"EVEN IF OUR EFFORTS OF ATTENTION
SEEM FOR YEARS TO BE PRODUCING
NO RESULT, ONE DAY A LIGHT THAT IS
IN EXACT PROPORTION TO THEM WILL
FLOOD THE SOUL."

~SIMONE WEIL

63

Okay, now, for some of you, the analogy to follow might make your head spin, but first humor me, hear me out, and then label me afflicted. For, boldly blossoming beneath this seemingly vague, yet calming blanket of wisdom, lays an avant-garde discovery of mind-altering proportion. Simply brush aside the purposeful fog to reveal the rays of righteous foreshadowing and enlightening promise.

Now, go ahead and re-read Weil's words. Clearly this isn't our parents' trite ending to the guilt-ridden soapbox of walking to school through the snow, barefoot, uphill both ways, to build character and appreciate the challenges of life. It doesn't preach that if we put our humbled heads down and put our noses to the grindstone, then someday the gods of blood-sweat-n-tears will ante up to that which we have desired, to finally put our fatigued little minds at ease.

It lovingly says just the opposite. Our faithfully steadfast focus, all-encompassing desirous planning and back-breaking labor may never yield that which we had our hearts set on as the Holy Grail of rewards. Our wants may outwittingly outweigh our efforts. And, even still, as we churn and burn to effect tangible results, the evidence may appear meager, if at all.

Alas, herein echoes the resounding lesson so eloquently crafted by poets and musicians alike: in all our work for wanting, we may still receive all that we really need.

Got it now? Such simple profundity blesses us with the equally unequivocal truth. Relentless pushing and production cannot, nor will ever, truly net enough fruits to sustain our hungry minds, hearts, and spirits. Instead, deciphering that which we want from that which we need garners new growth, not only in our pursuits, but also in our methods of calculating and conquering. When we resolve to acknowledge, respect, and ultimately honor this gratuitous salvation, the old habits wither away. In turn, we clear the weeds of bitter-sweetness and allow our gardens to flourish with light, life, love, and learning.

"BEING HAPPY DOESN'T MEAN EVERYTHING'S PERFECT. IT MEANS YOU'VE DECIDED TO SEE BEYOND THE IMPERFECTIONS."

~ANONYMOUS

64

Relax and open your mind to embrace and absorb this overtly fundamental, yet life-saving concept of candor. Grab hold of its depth and pour a pitcher of happiness in acceptance of your current reality. Then wade into the flood of prompting prose and choose tidal change over drowning correction.

Create bolder. Rescue braver. Shine brighter.
Explore broader. Relax calmer. Fight cleaner.
Speak clearer. Follow closer. Lounge cooler.

Breathe deeper. Save earlier. Travel farther.
Run faster. Dream fiercer. Commit firmer.
Pray forever. Trust freer. Retreat fresher.

Laugh fuller. Befriend gentler. Celebrate grander.
Think greener. Cook healthier. Practice harder.
Fly higher. Treat kinder. Donate larger.

Stay up later. Eat leaner. Pack lighter.
Sleep longer. Hang looser. Sing louder.
Write neater. Play nicer. Walk prouder.

Forgive quicker. Preach quieter. Share richer.
Drive safer. Dress sharper. Plan simpler.
Chew slower. Owe smaller. Discipline softer.

Reply sooner. Aim straighter. Sweat stricter.
Kiss sweeter. Serve swifter. Stand taller.
Hug tighter. Lavish thicker. Build tougher.

Perform truer. Touch warmer. Smile wider.
Dance wilder. Spend wiser. Act younger.
Work smarter. Feel stronger. Look better. Live longer.

"REMEMBER, THE LIGHT AT THE END OF
THE TUNNEL MAY BE YOU."

~STEVEN TYLER, *AEROSMITH*

Ahhh, there's nothing quite like a full helping of delicious profundity and irony to fill your belly. Today's lesson emerges to lead you through a colorful picture show to an extreme close-up with reality. And I'll cut right to the chase. Picture a bull's eye, ringed with the boldness of luring aim, hovering smack dab over the center of your chest. See it. Feel it. Trust that it's there because it points to your soul.

Now, regardless of your beliefs in who or what created you, and how or why you appeared on the big screen, you are here. Period. Whether through your very own Big Bang theory of Jane and John Doe, the renowned stork, or a god of your naming and omnipotent standing, you've been duly delivered. And undeniably planted deep within your body revs a little generator, hard-wired with a zestful yearning to live and learn and love. Amidst the blessings and curses of an unpredictable storyline, though, this unflickering energy faces but one formidable challenge: Your wavering belief in its undying power.

When high times flourish, your reliance on people, places, and things for sustenance is ostensibly overshadowed. Fueled by and following your glowing golden spark, it might even appear that good fortune were simply part of the sketch, written as such with or without your character taking the reins. The needs of your body and mind met by a delivering spirit.

Conversely, loom the myriad situations when the lesser of two evils shows up at your front door, when a worst case scenario unfolds before your very eyes, or when the tides of hell *and* high water flood your path. Oftentimes, you inadvertently discount your own power and look outside yourself for a lifeline of salvation. As you gravitate to the center of yourself in weary deliberation, you now see the tribulations overshadow your light, and you believe any eventual reemergence will not be born of your own power.

Perhaps *today* is the day, then, that you examine yourself through another lens.

Perhaps in tough times your saving grace has been merely a pulse and a prayer, but still you pulled yourself through the muck and mire. No doubt, standing in soliloquy and without script in hand nor knight in shining armor, *you* put the brakes on worrying, whining, and wishing, and made things happen with *you*, for *you*, because of *you*, and only when *you* were ready. Meaning, folks, that the entrenched engine within your chest never did let you down—you simply forgot its infinitely redeeming power. In essence, *you* were the very light at the end of the tunnel.

And so I charge you to reexamine your target and awaken your own sleeping giant. When you elect to aim for the light, the abyss of questions and doubt, fear and flight, seem to fall from periphery, and clarity and clairvoyance emerge to radiate. Purposefully recharge your batteries. Refocus your energies. Rekindle your spirit for both elation and submission. And rediscover your given gifts of grace, glory, and glee. For, regardless of your rite of passage, be it science, stork, or Savior, you have a scintillating soul and a story for survival.

"You're still here? It's over. Go home."

~Ferris Bueller

About the Author

Kimberlie Dykeman is one of those people you don't soon forget. If her smile and laugh don't get you first, her energy will. She is a woman on a mission. And her passion is overflowing, if not contagious. She has dedicated her life to being a motivator, entertainer, and educator; and whether on-camera, on-air, on the field, or on paper, Kimberlie exudes a charismatic, vivacious presence that has fueled a loyal following and countless success stories. Her industry expertise, business savvy, and professional etiquette command attention and respect as a renowned TV and Multimedia Personality and Producer, Motivational Lifestyle Coach and Wellness Expert, International Spokesperson, and Author. Yet it's her unique blend of natural curiosity, engaging charm, and entertaining wit that allows her to interactively connect with and captivate any audience.

Kimberlie grew up on the beautiful rural outskirts of Rhinebeck, New York, and earned a degree in Literature & Rhetoric from Binghamton University. Though she cherished the comforts of a small-town community, Kimberlie had her sights set on making it big and exploring the rest of the world . Determined to build her own career path from the simple concept of helping people live life to its fullest, fittest, and finest, she traveled throughout the United States and logged a gamut of entrepreneurial experiences, from elite personal trainer and lifestyle expert columnist to model and stand-up comic. Capitalizing on this diverse palate, Kimberlie emerged as self-proclaimed Lifestyle Coach and, in 1999, set up shop in Austin, Texas, to pioneer a groundbreaking system of executive coaching. Through her private practice, InnerStrength Connection, Kimberlie evolved into a motivational speaker, multimedia wellness expert, and health news correspondent, earning her recognition as one of Austin's "Thought Leaders." And, her unyielding commitment to the written word transformed her nationally broadcasted inspirational email, The Monday Soapbox Edition, into the book you are holding today.

Oh, but Kimberlie's vision just kept on growing, prompting her to tap the power of mass media and the Internet. Pairing her rugged street smarts with the support of a talented advisory team, she took on the City of Angels in 2005 to officially launch what has become conglomerate multimedia entity. As an on-camera personality and producer, she has blazed a bold path through the world of global entertainment and promotion, seizing every opportunity to entertain, enlighten, and uplift millions of viewers.

In her young life, Kimberlie has indeed built a loyal following and worn many hats. Television and multimedia maven, coach, author, athlete, community leader.

In the end, though, they all look the same on her. She is a motivator, entertainer, and educator for our times. A woman on a mission.

To learn more about *Pure Soapbox* and subscribe to SOAPBOX™ visit www.puresoapbox.com

For more information about Kimberlie Dykeman visit www.kimberliedykeman.com

Contact by email: info@puresoapbox.com